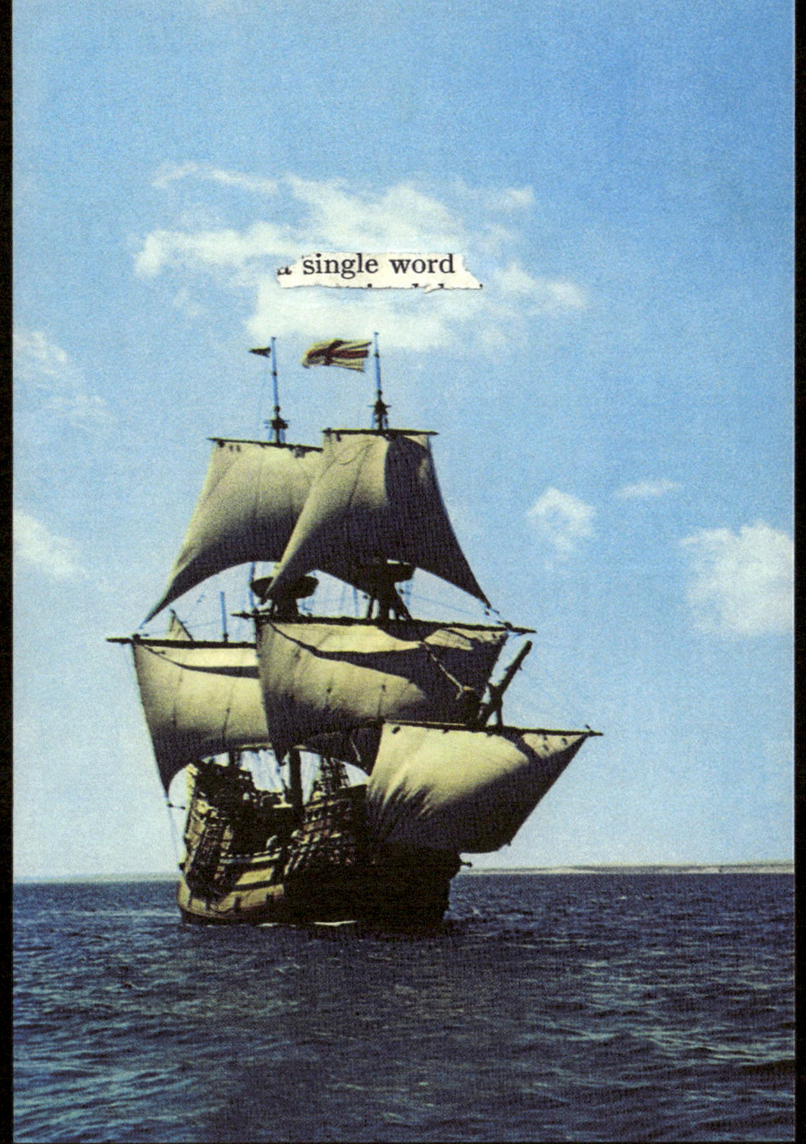

SEEKING FROZEN SOUND

PostCardPoems

CLARK LUNBERRY

SEEKING FROZEN SOUND
by Clark Lunberry

Copyright © 2023 by Clark Lunberry
Published by Tofu Ink Arts Press. All rights reserved.
Cover & book design by JLTY Atelier

ISBN: 978-1-958661-10-9

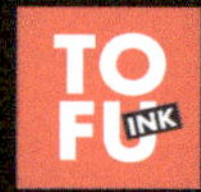

Tofu Ink Arts Press, a celebratory venture, aims at publishing poems and other arts of un humdrum'd inclusive rhizomatic errant possibilities. We support polished work of established & emerging poets and artists that are absorbed in possibilities. We are committed to amplifying voices of the under-represented and marginalized.
Art makes you think about thinking…
ABSORB POSSIBILITIES!

www.TOFUINK.com
A member of CLMP

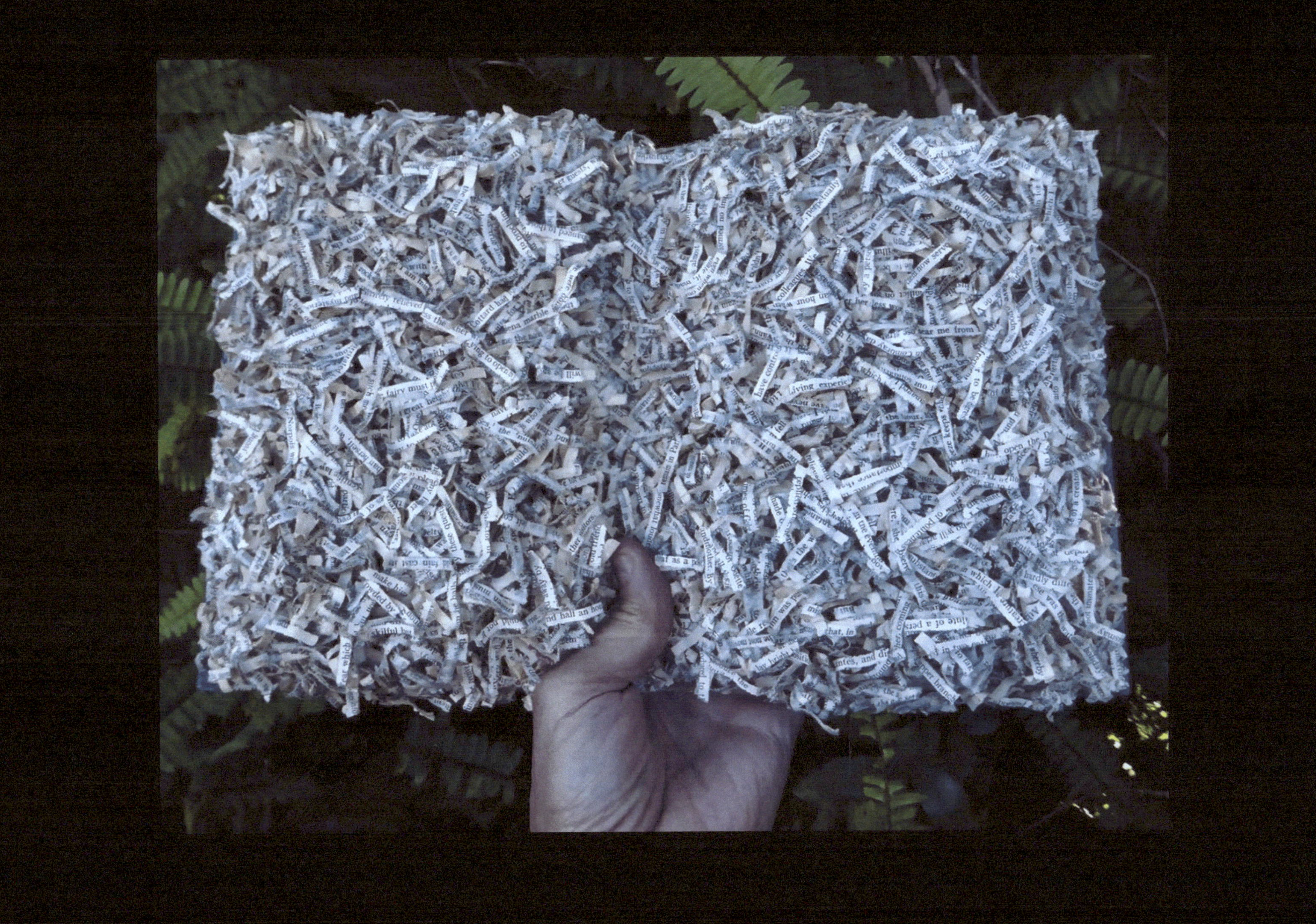

FOREWORD

"We have of the universe only formless, fragmentary visions, which we complete by the association of arbitrary ideas, creating dangerous suggestions."
—Marcel Proust

My father, Dale Lunberry (1927-2012), was a jeweler and watchmaker in a small town in Kansas, the place where I grew up. For decades, when traveling, always with his wife, my mother, Barbara Lunberry (1929-2002), he often purchased travel postcards of the various places visited. These hundreds of postcards (more than 750) were, as far as I know, never sent to anyone through the mail, and were instead collected and later carefully catalogued, as souvenirs, perhaps as a means of remembering the many places they had been.

Rarely is anything written on the backs of these postcards (my father was a man of few words), however, there might occasionally be seen a brief inscription (in my father's unmistakable handwriting) of the date on which the place on the postcard was visited: "6-26-63," "Apr. 7, 74," "8-19-64," or, at most, for a particular Hawaiian hotel, "Here 3 days Jan 21-24, 83."

At my father's death in 2012, I inherited his box of postcards, but I was uncertain of what I would ever do with it (though reluctant to throw it away, as so much else had been thrown away). So, I held onto the box, placing it in a closet, mostly forgetting about it.

One day during the spring of 2020, with COVID's arrival, and the consequences of suddenly spending so much time at home (and, importantly, of not traveling), I got the box of travel postcards out of the closet and began casually sorting through them. Picking out those cards that were particularly striking or strange, often oddly beautiful, I was drawn to how so many of the colorful pictures vividly spoke of other times, other places (with, for instance, the characteristic blues of the postcard skies offering a mid-century modern variant of the poeticized French azure).

While those who were anonymously photographed in the postcards (walking on sidewalks, standing on street corners, lounging on a sandy beach…) reminded me of that which, though obvious, is often overlooked—that postcards are indeed photographs. And as photographs (with space on their opposite sides intended for written messages), I recalled Susan Sontag's description of how "…all photographs are *memento mori*. To take a photograph is to participate in another person's (or thing's) mortality, vulnerability, mutability. Precisely by slicing out this moment and freezing it, all photographs testify to time's relentless melt." The (forgotten) photography of the postcard is no exception to that poignant revelation, presenting in the printed picture perhaps its otherwise deferred and unwritten message.

At about the same time that I was rediscovering my father's postcards, I stumbled upon (largely by accident) ways in which small fragments from a copy of Marcel Proust's *Remembrance of Things Past* (shredded for another project that I was working on) could at times be provocatively placed directly on the postcards, glued into the image. As a kind of poetically clandestine caption, or as a fissuring mark of dislocating intervention, Proust's broken lines of language were suddenly seen as if commenting upon their estranged new setting. There, his words of remembrance were now newly remembering, as if onto the postcard's photographic surface, into its space of things past, "where thinking," as Walter Benjamin noted of photography, "suddenly stops in a constellation saturated with tensions."

To my pleasure and surprise, and before I knew it, my postcard project had taken on a life of its own, offering even a means of imaginative travel (in time, in place), while also allowing a collaboration of sorts with my deceased father, and of an engagement with Proustian memory, from my father's own past, my own present, and of our own time together, and apart.

...on hearing the language of

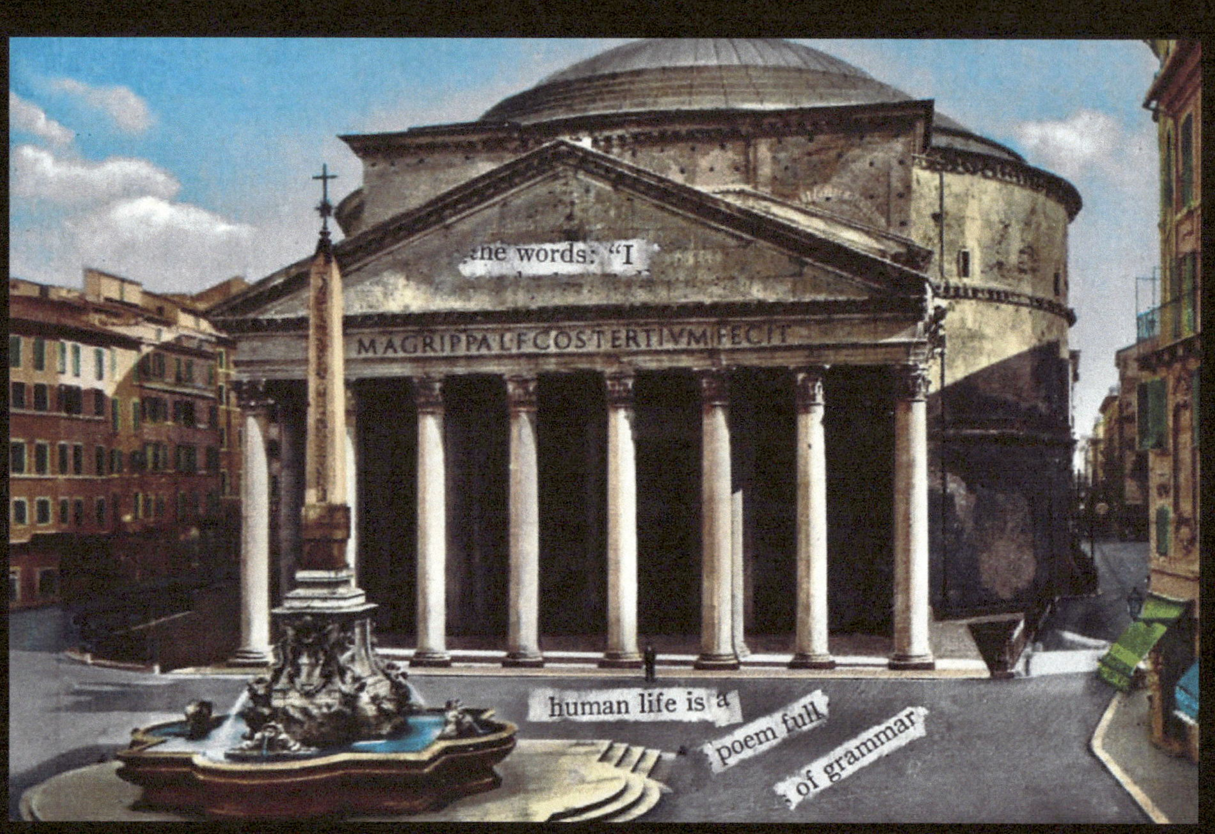
ne words: "I
MAGRIPPA·L·F·COS·TERTIVM·FECIT
human life is a
poem full
of grammar

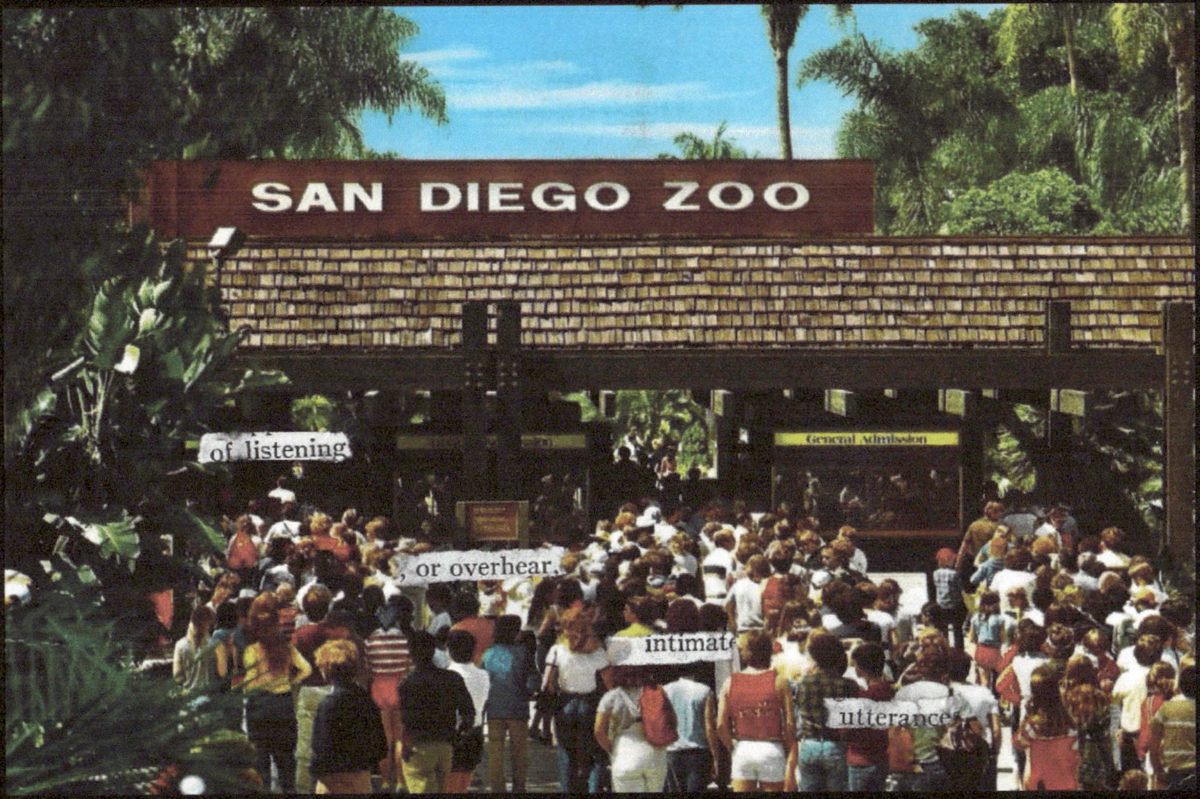

SAN DIEGO ZOO
General Admission
of listening
, or overhear,
intimate
utterance

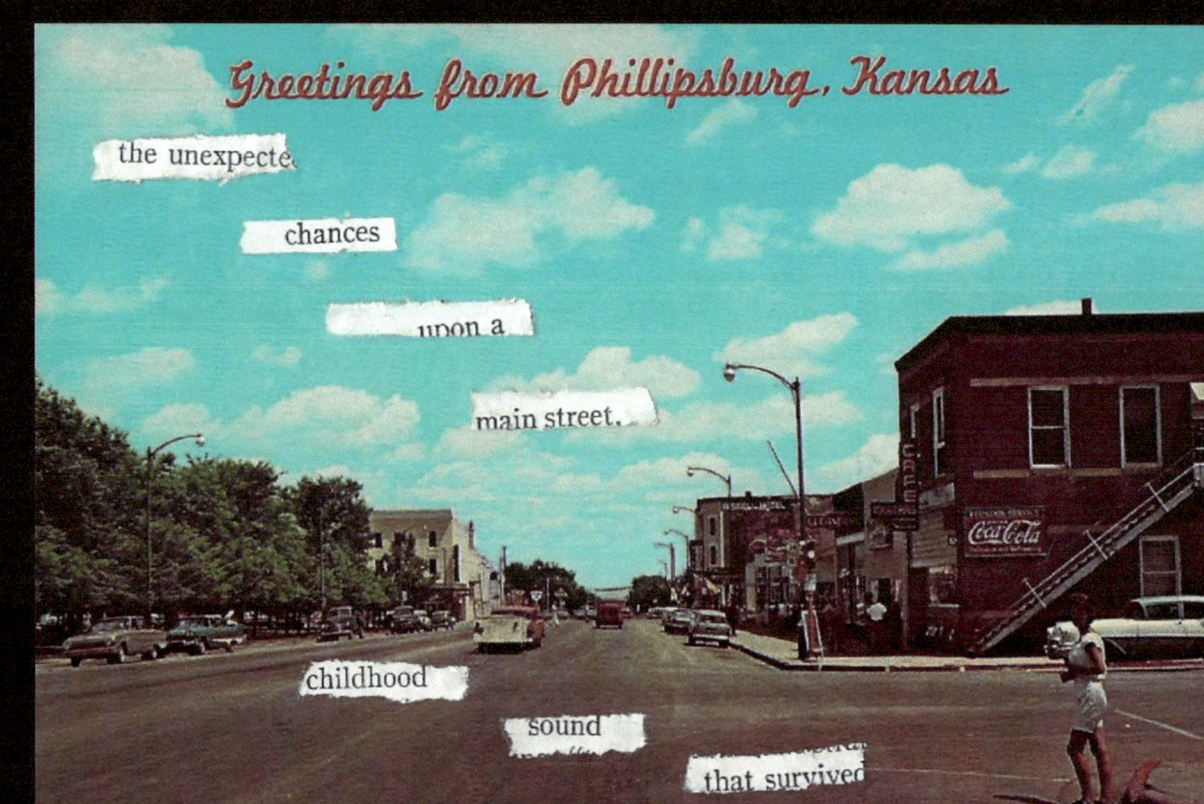
Greetings from Phillipsburg, Kansas
the unexpected
chances
upon a
main street,
childhood
sound
that survived

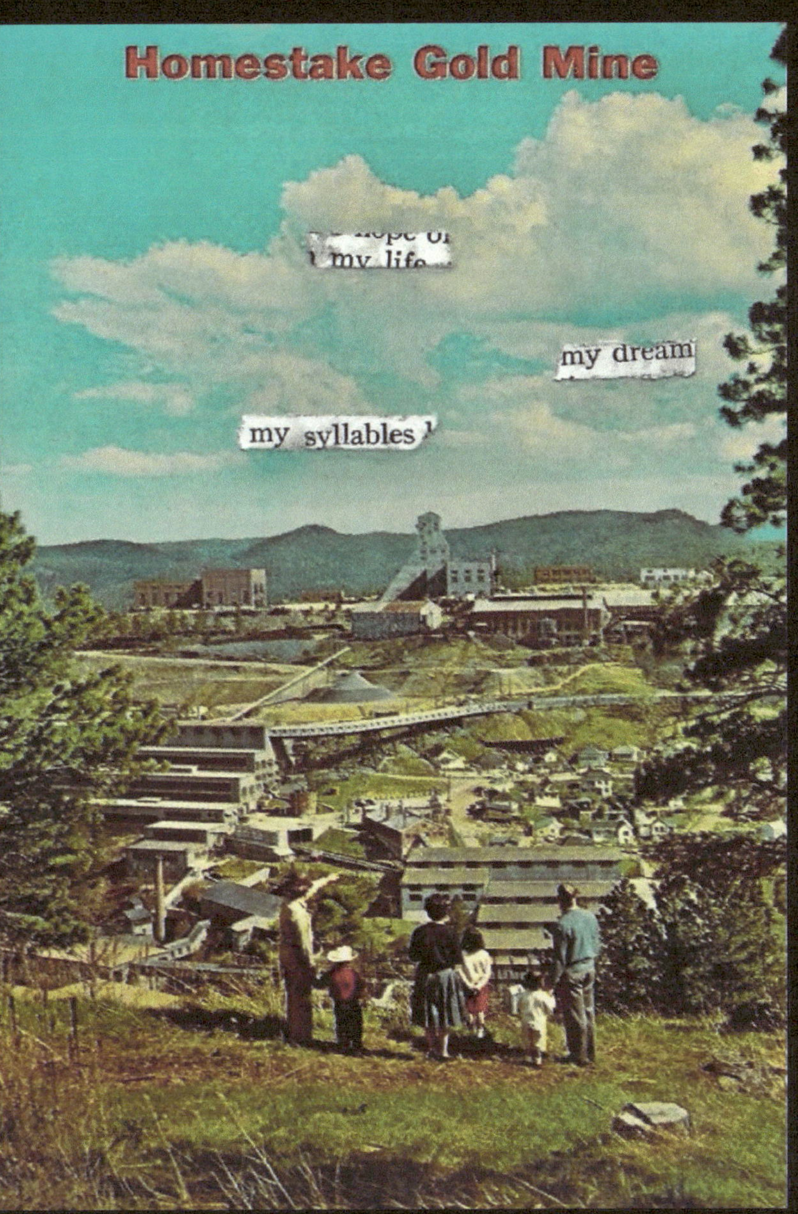
Homestake Gold Mine
hope of
my life
my dream
my syllables

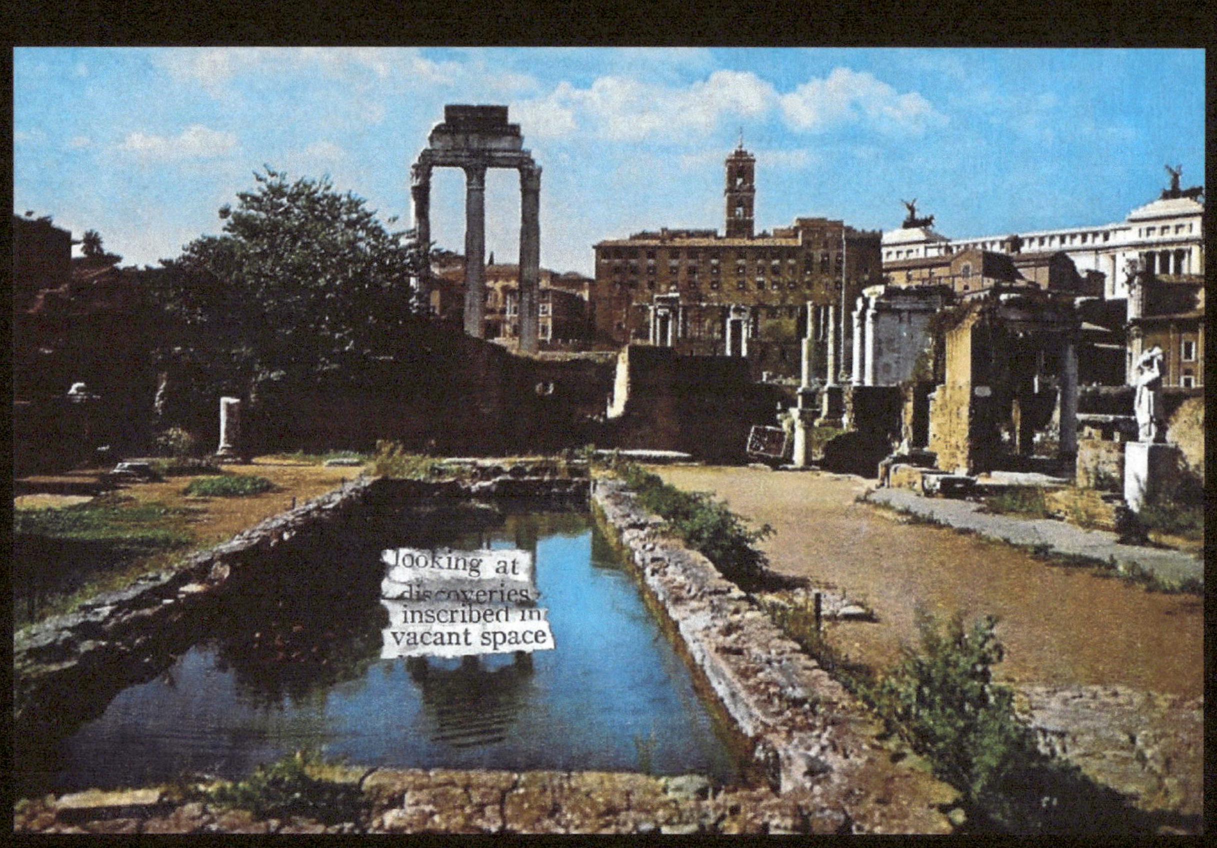
looking at
discoveries
inscribed in
vacant space

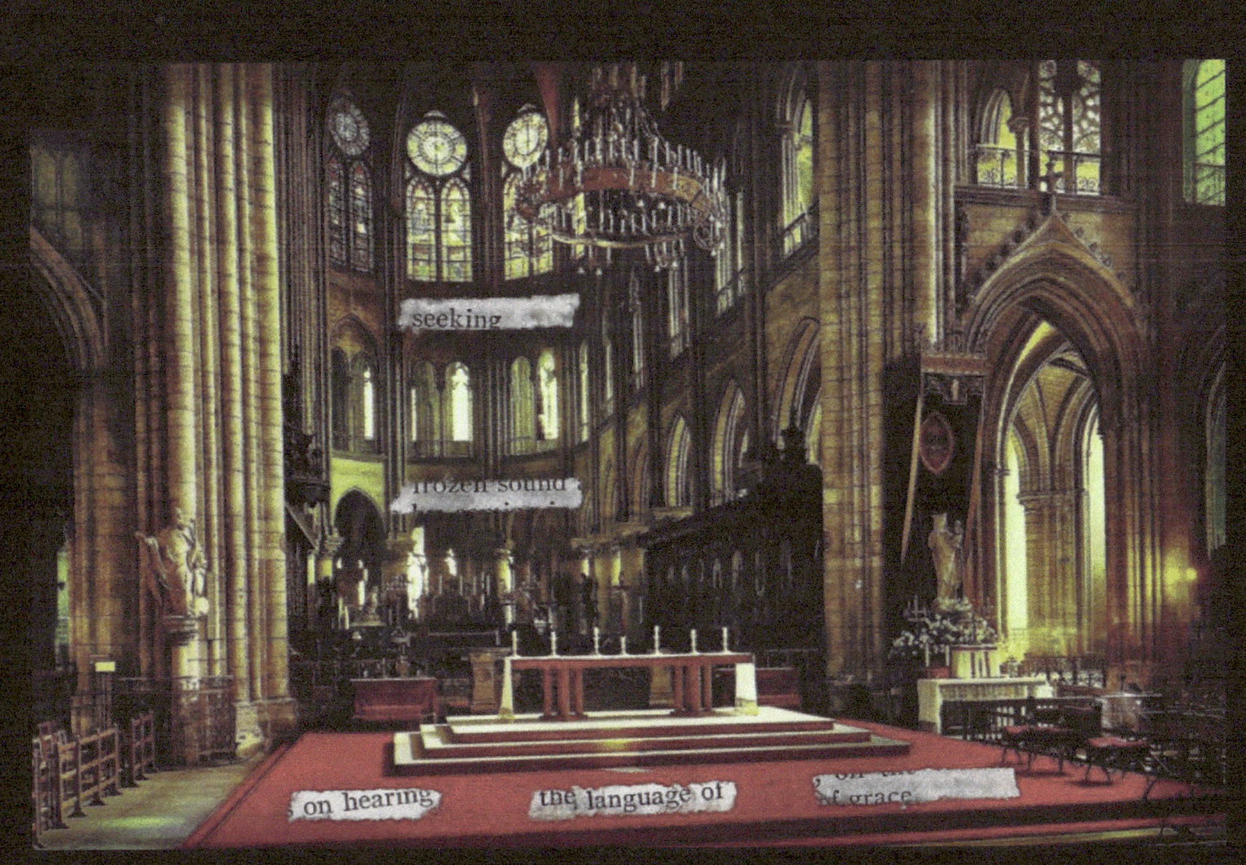
seeking
frozen sound
on hearing
the language of
of grace

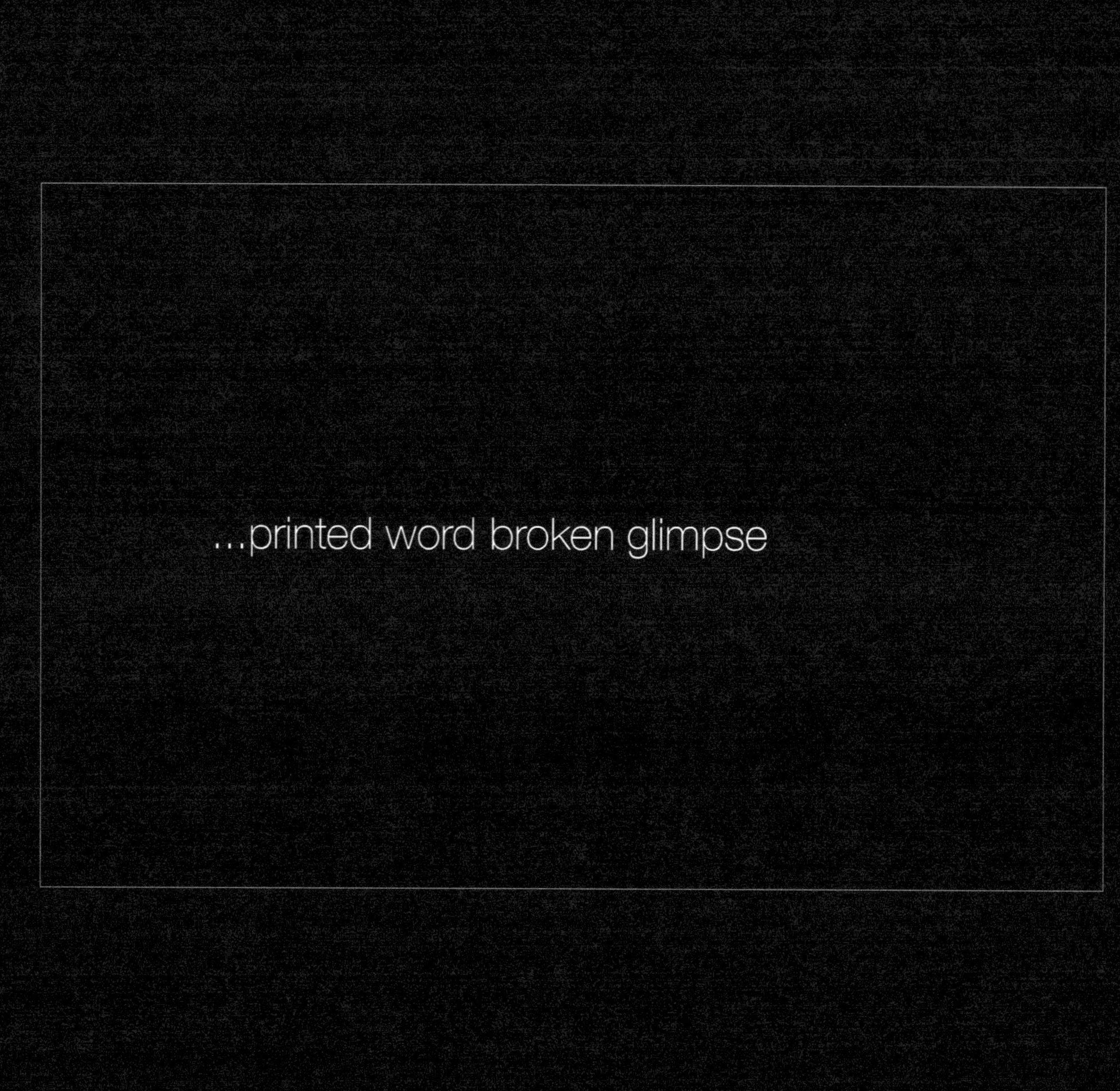
...printed word broken glimpse

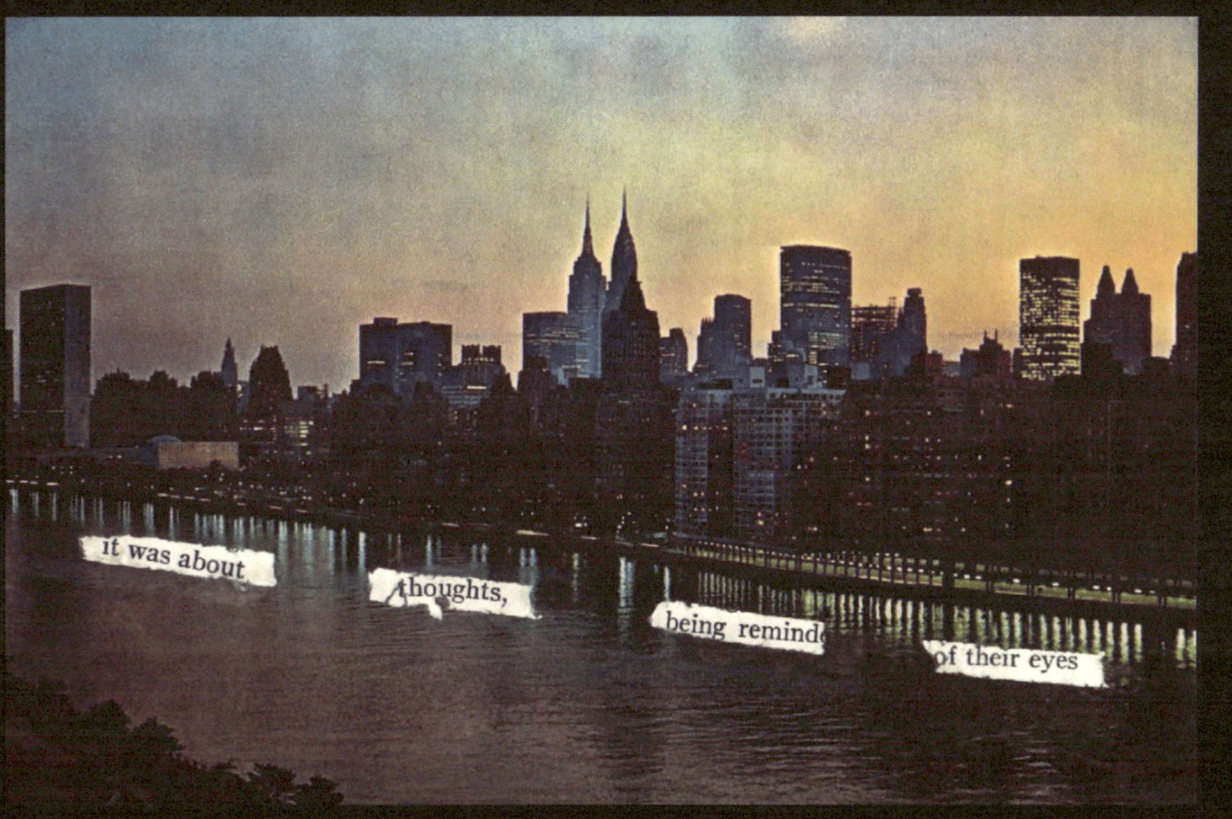
it was about
thoughts,
being reminde
of their eyes

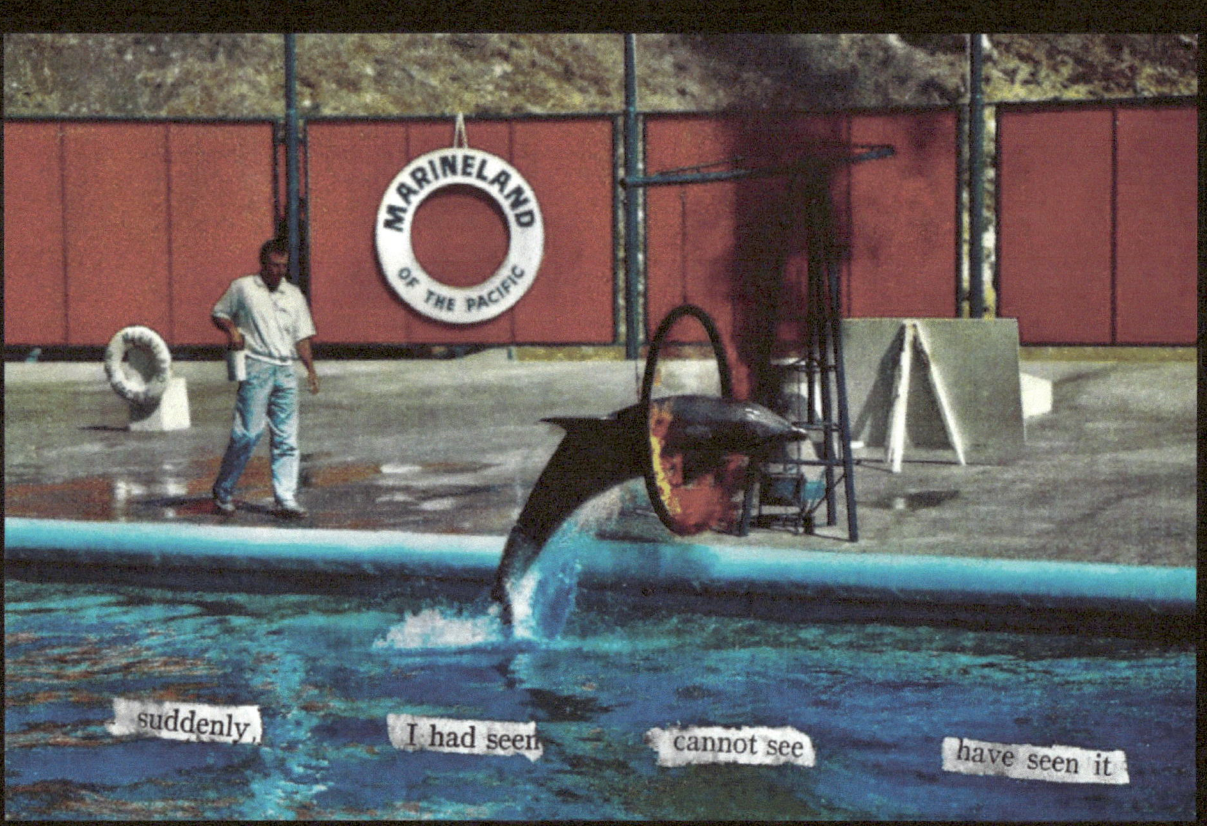

MARINELAND
OF THE PACIFIC
suddenly,
I had seen
cannot see
have seen it

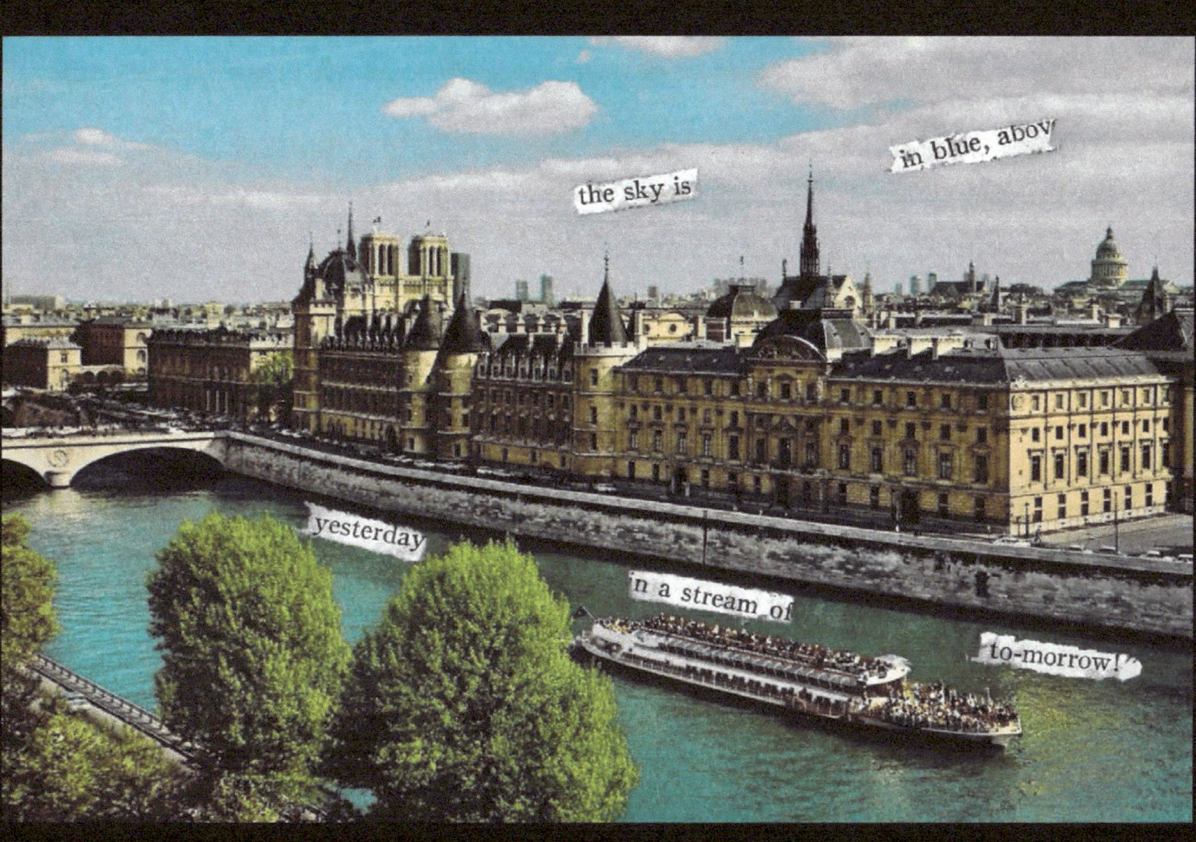

the sky is
in blue, abov
yesterday
in a stream of
to-morrow!

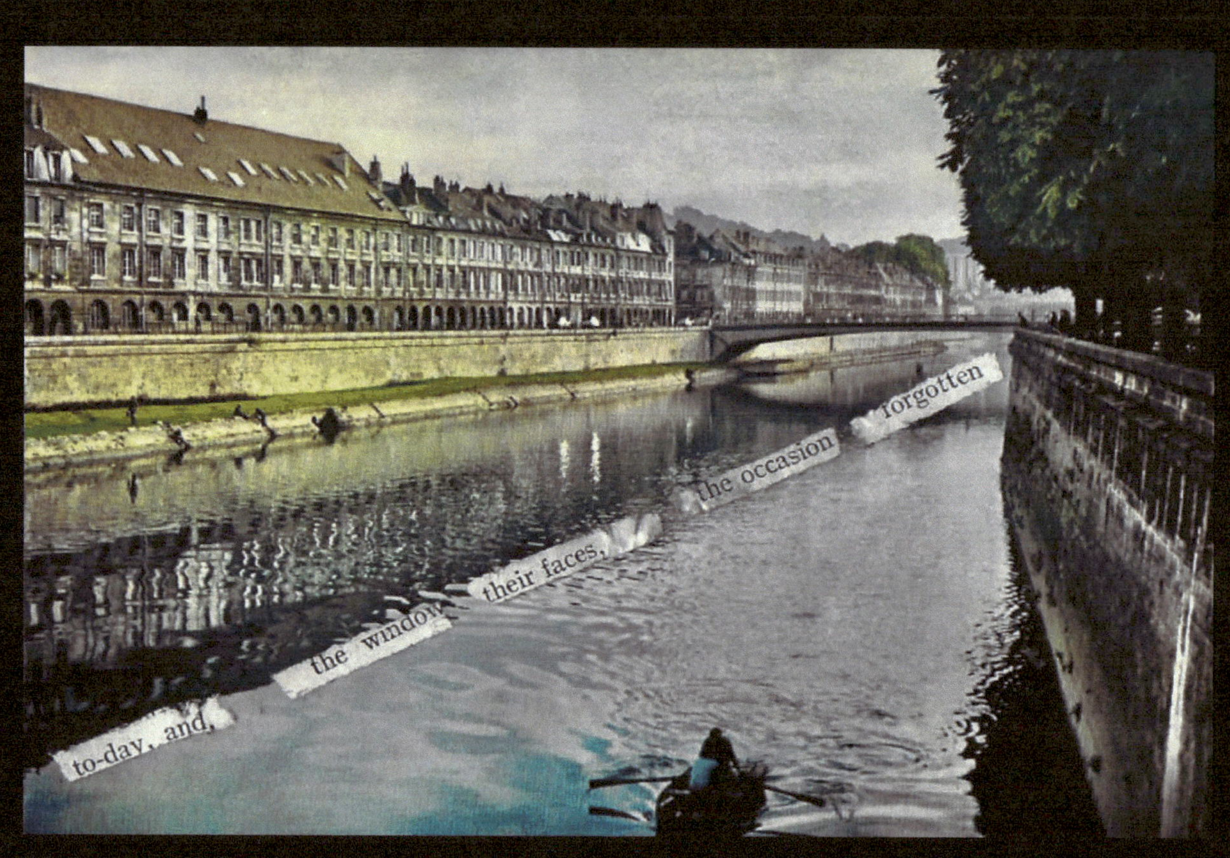
to-day, and,
the window
their faces,
the occasion
forgotten

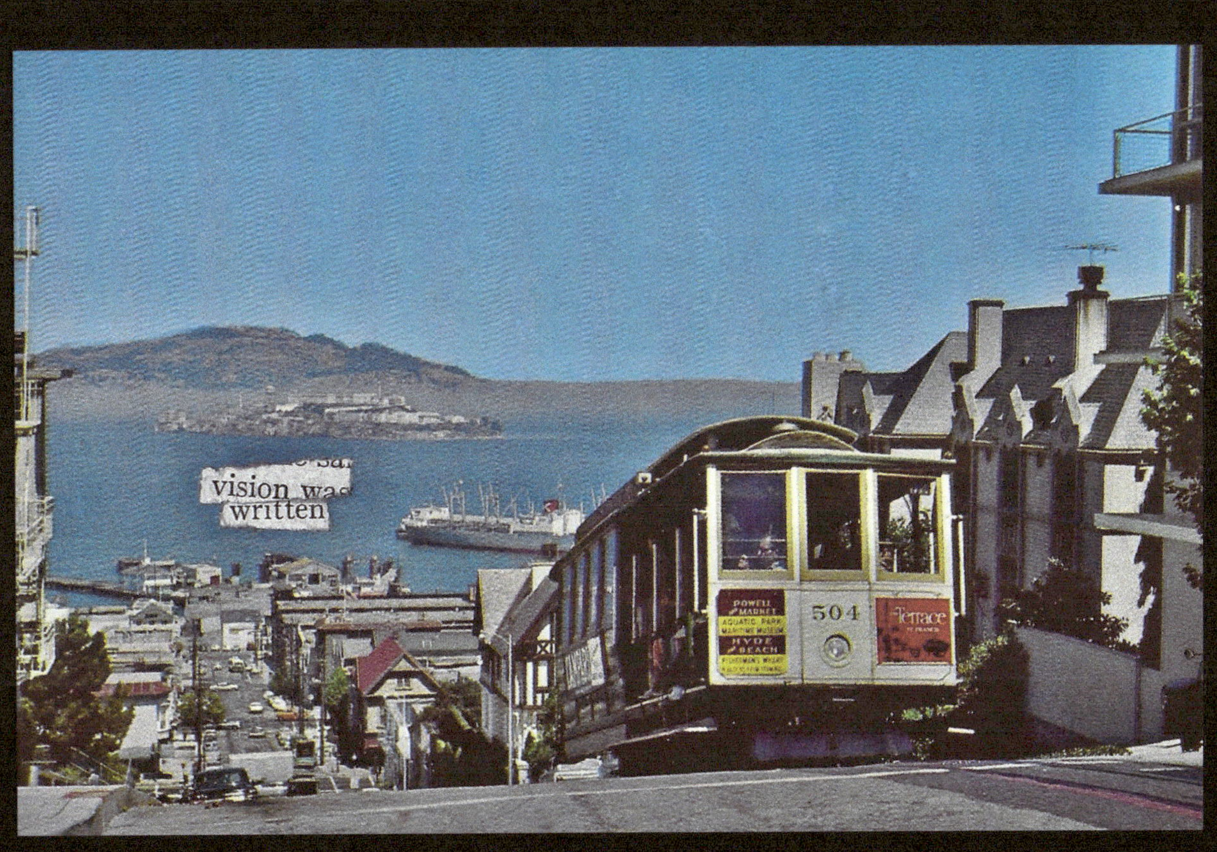

vision was
written
504
POWELL
MARKET
AQUATIC PARK
MARITIME MUSEUM
HYDE
BEACH
Terrace

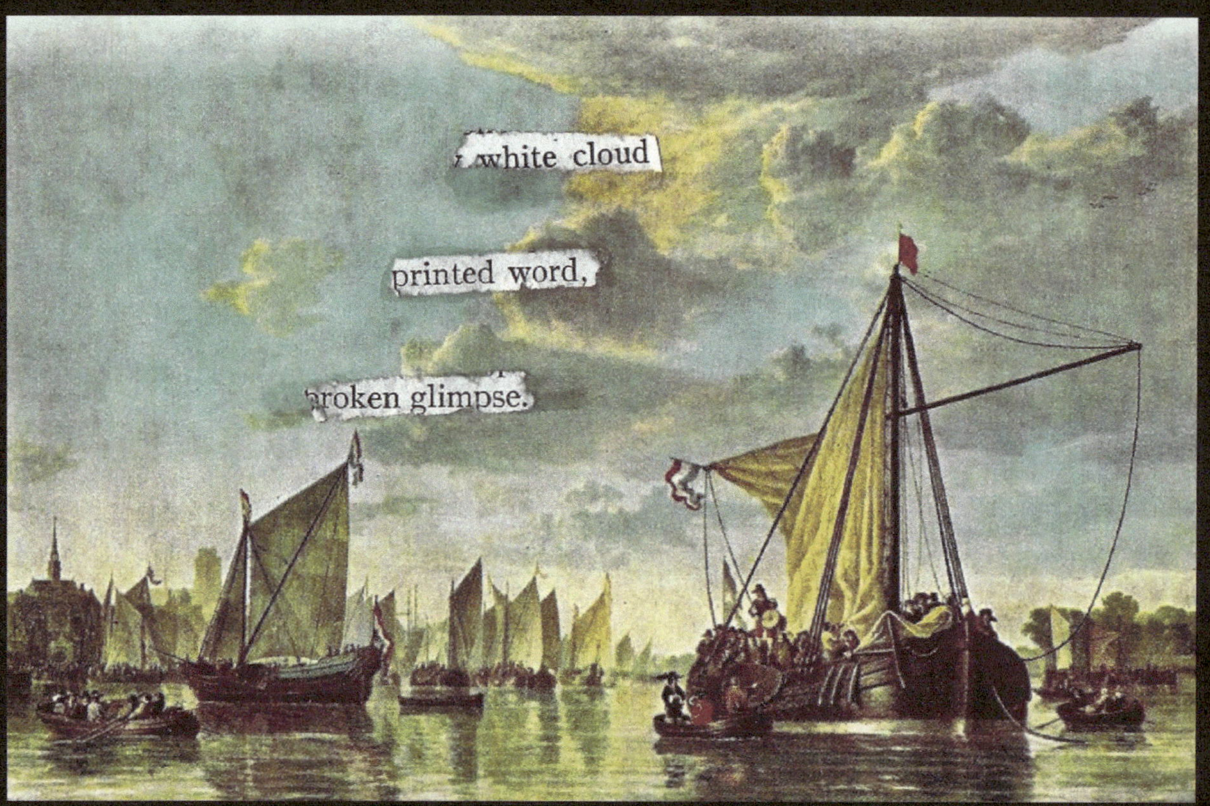
white cloud
printed word,
broken glimpse.

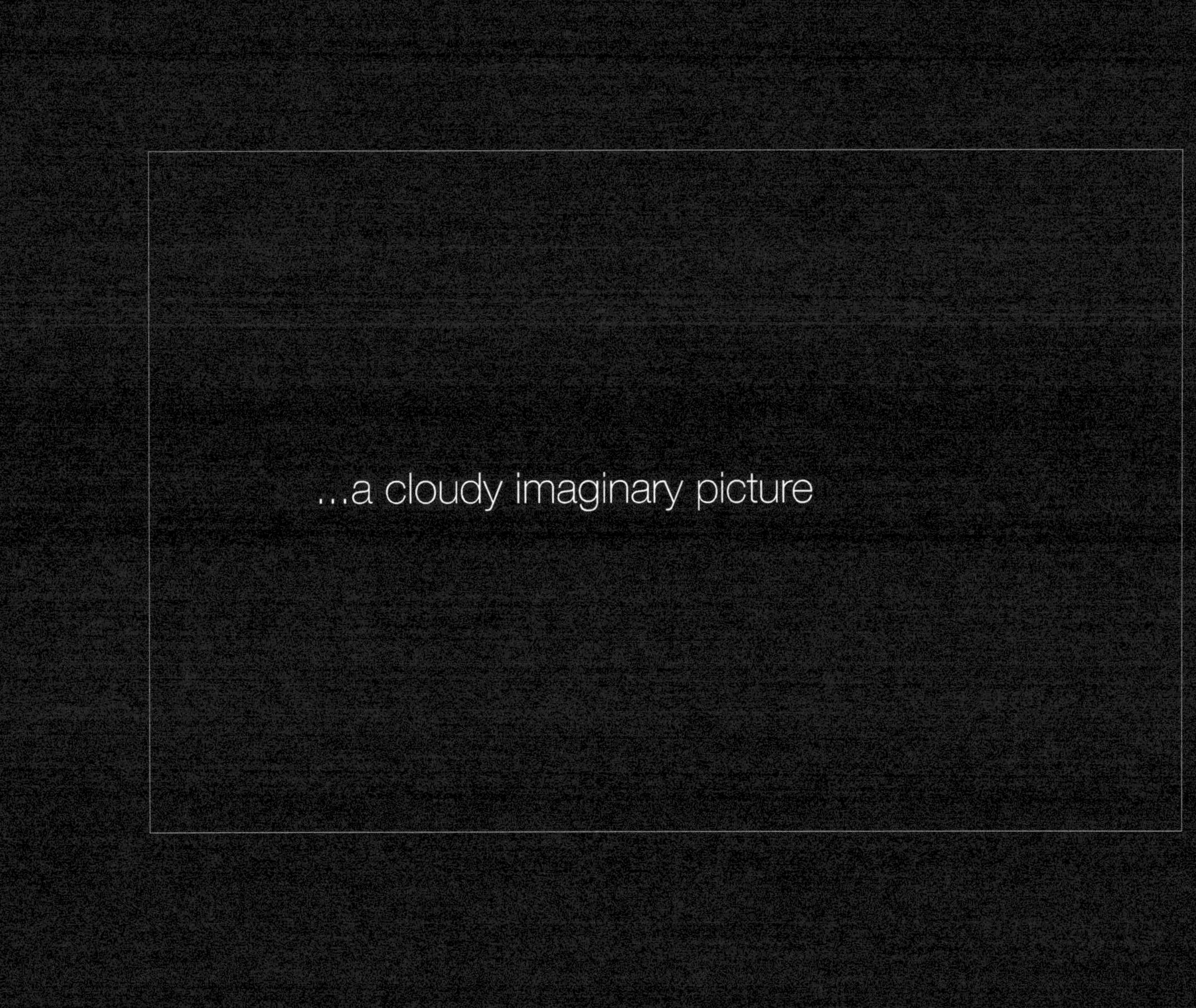
...a cloudy imaginary picture

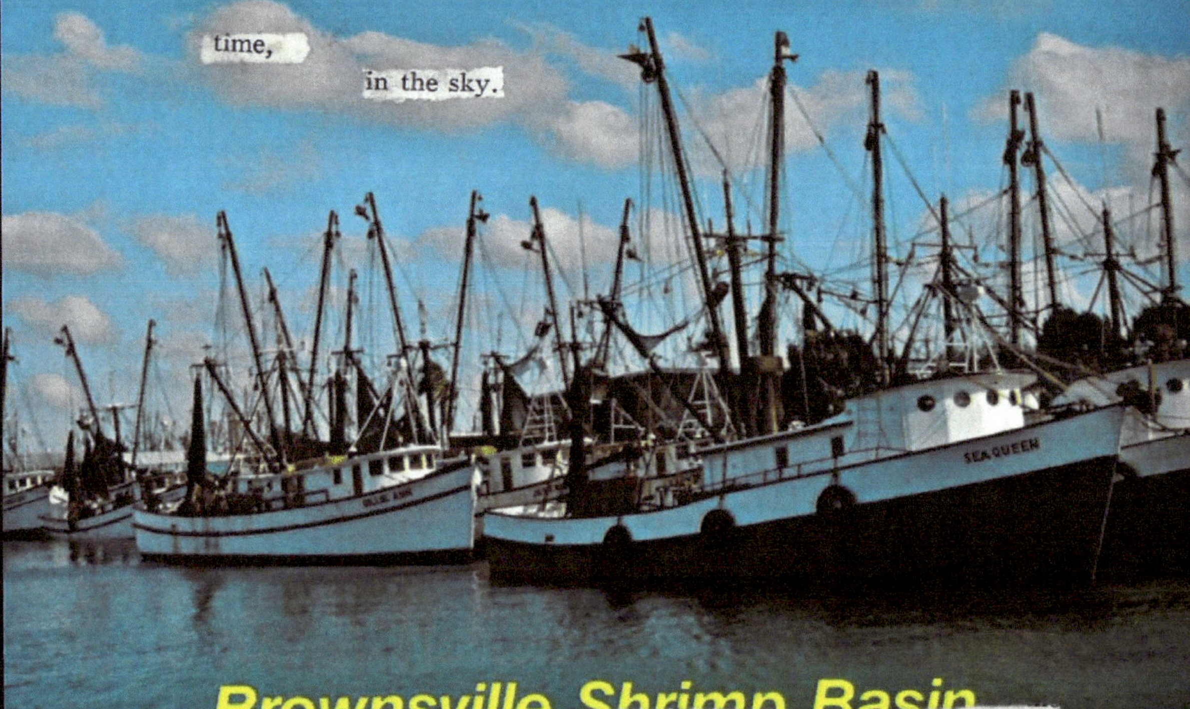

time,
in the sky.
Brownsville Shrimp Basin
suddenly
a certain clarity
began to trembl.
SEA QUEEN

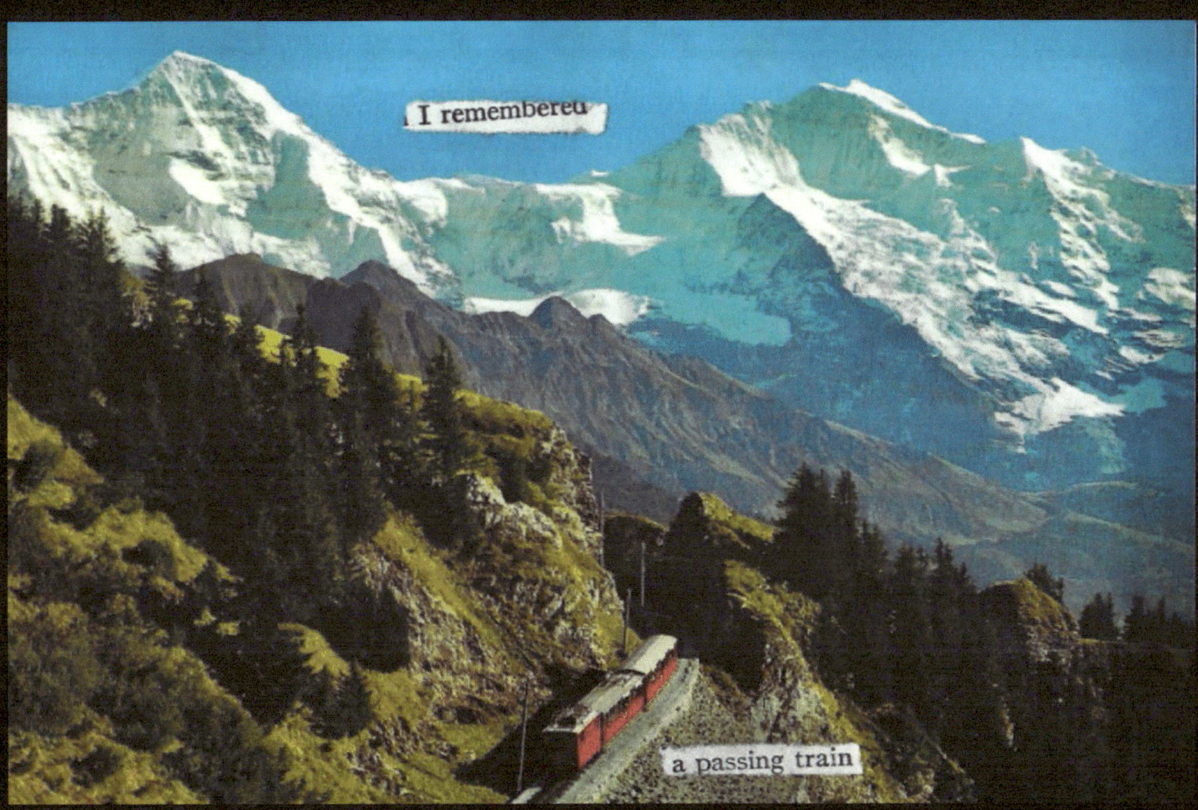
I remembered
a passing train

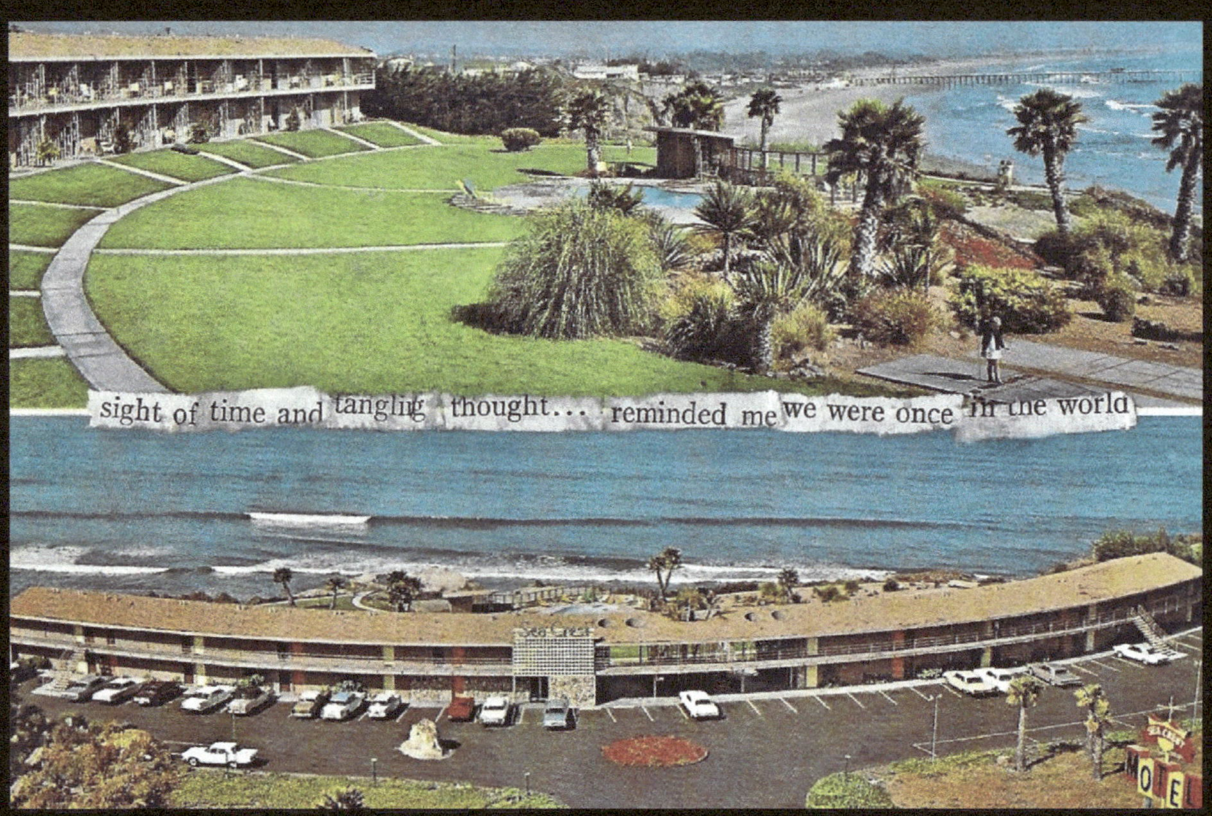

sight of time and tangling thought... reminded me we were once in the world

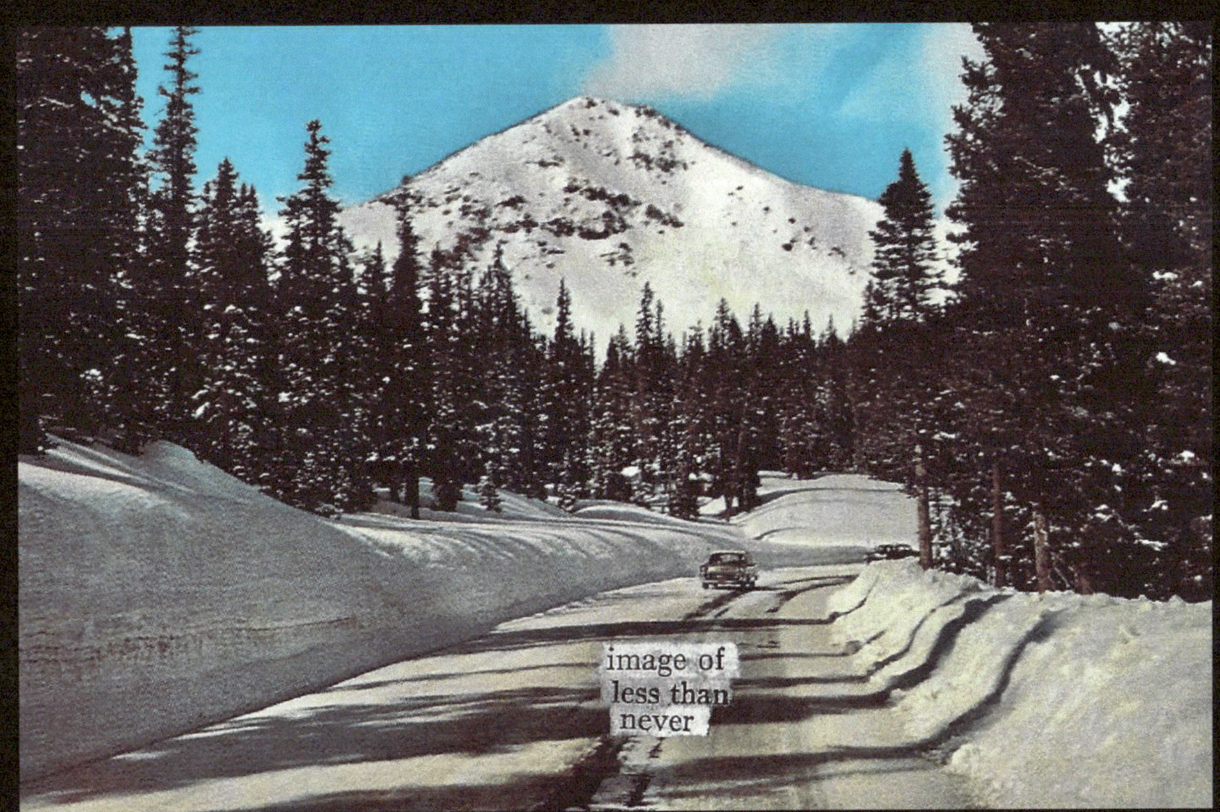

image of
less than
never

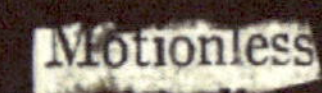
Motionless
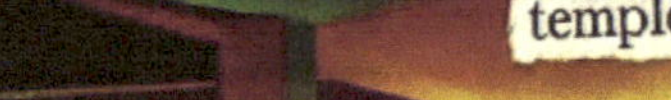
temple of

memory
Holiday Inn

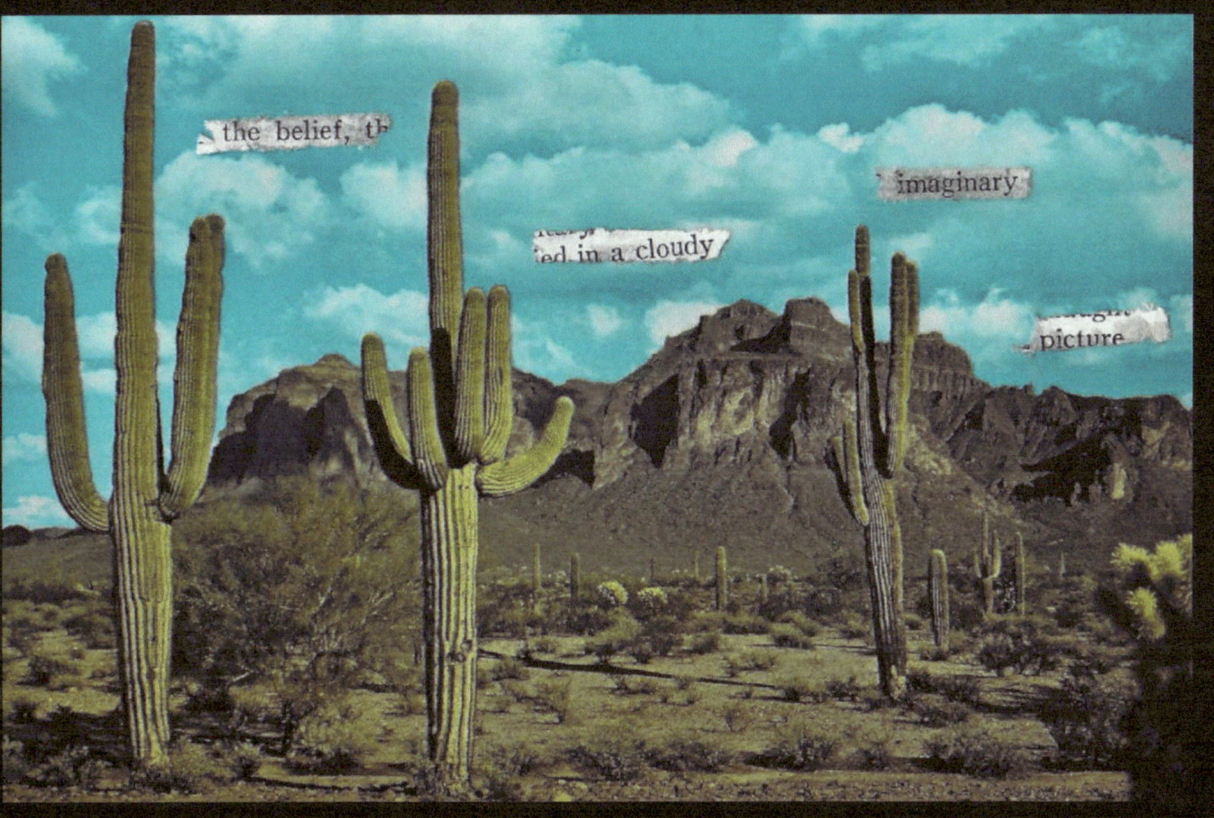
the belief, th
imaginary
ed in a cloudy
picture

...pronounce the photograph

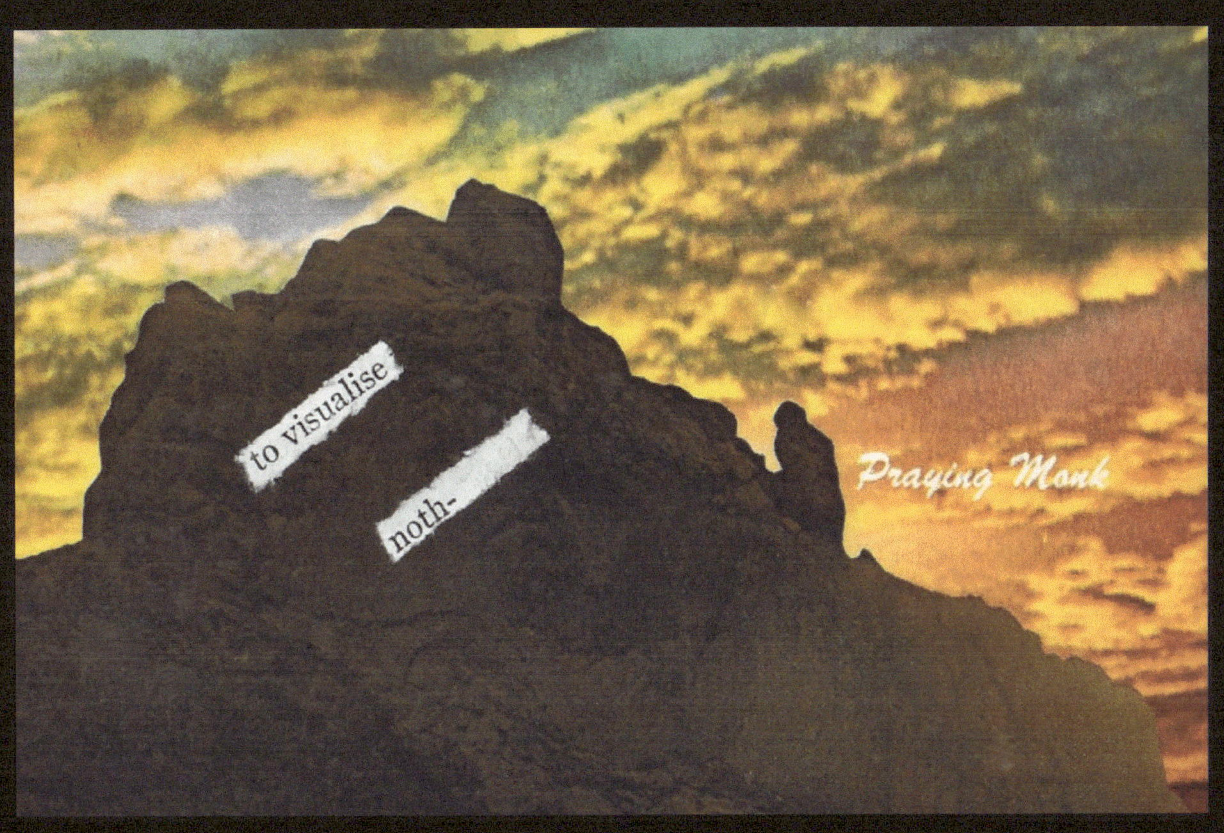

to visualise
noth-
Praying Monk

not a word.
immediate
note of a bird
"Remember
afterward
to have been
self had already
our eyes
the sight

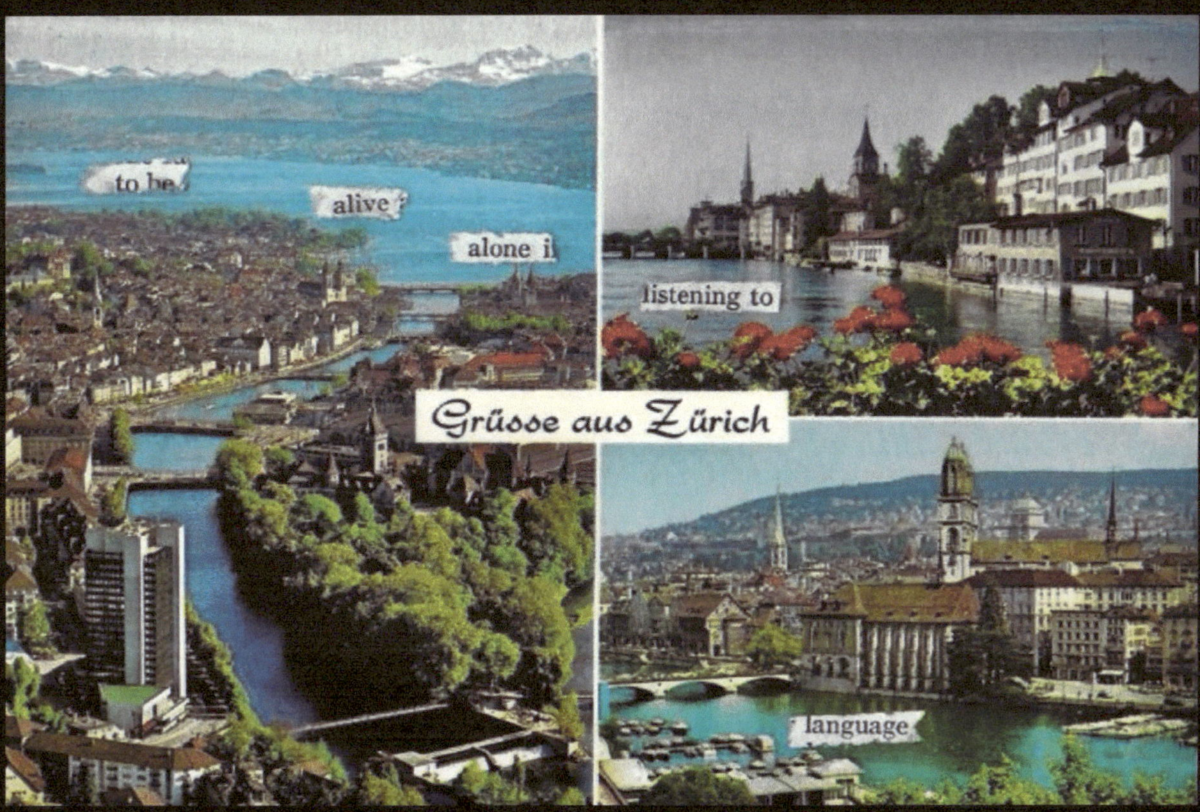
to be
alive
alone i
listening to
Grüsse aus Zürich
language

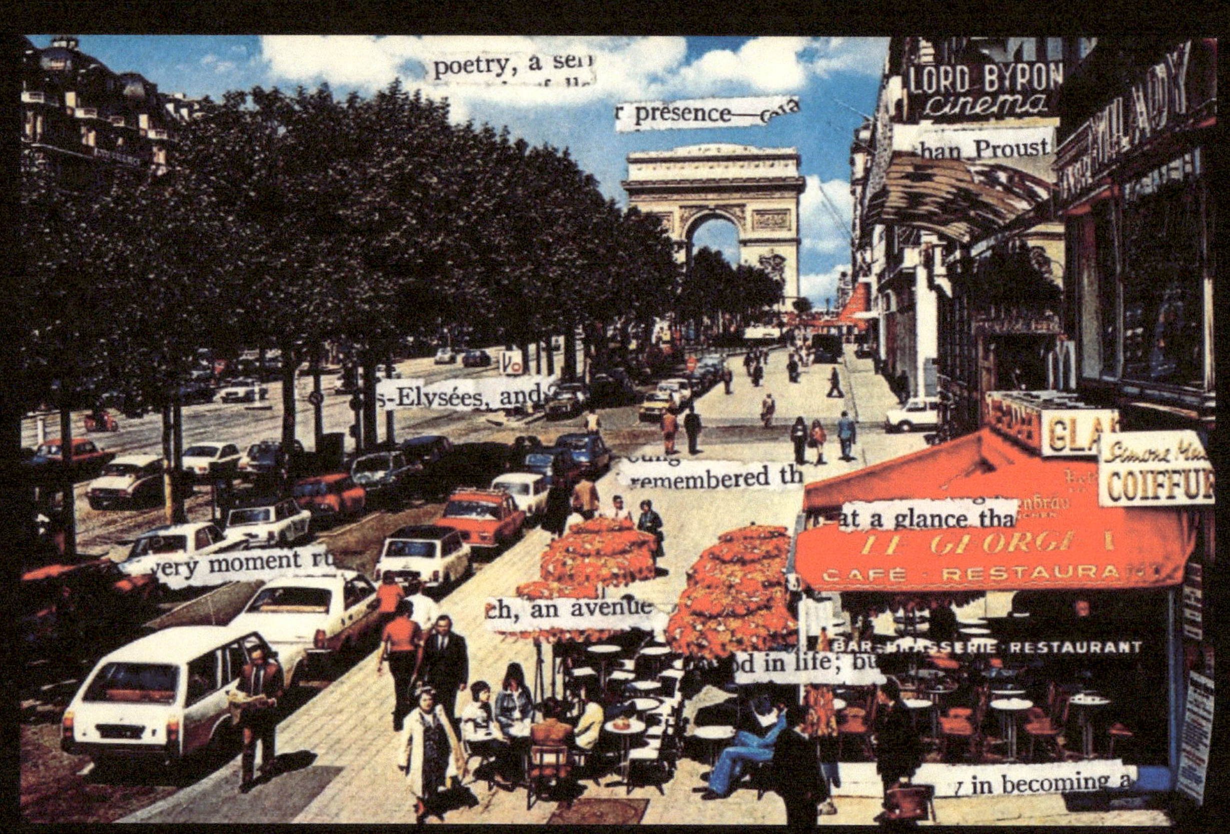

poetry, a sen
r presence—
s-Elysées, and
remembered th
very moment ru
at a glance tha
ch, an avenue
od in life; bu
in becoming a
LORD BYRON
cinema
han Proust
GLA
COIFFU
LE GEORGE I
CAFÉ · RESTAURANT
BAR · BRASSERIE · RESTAURANT

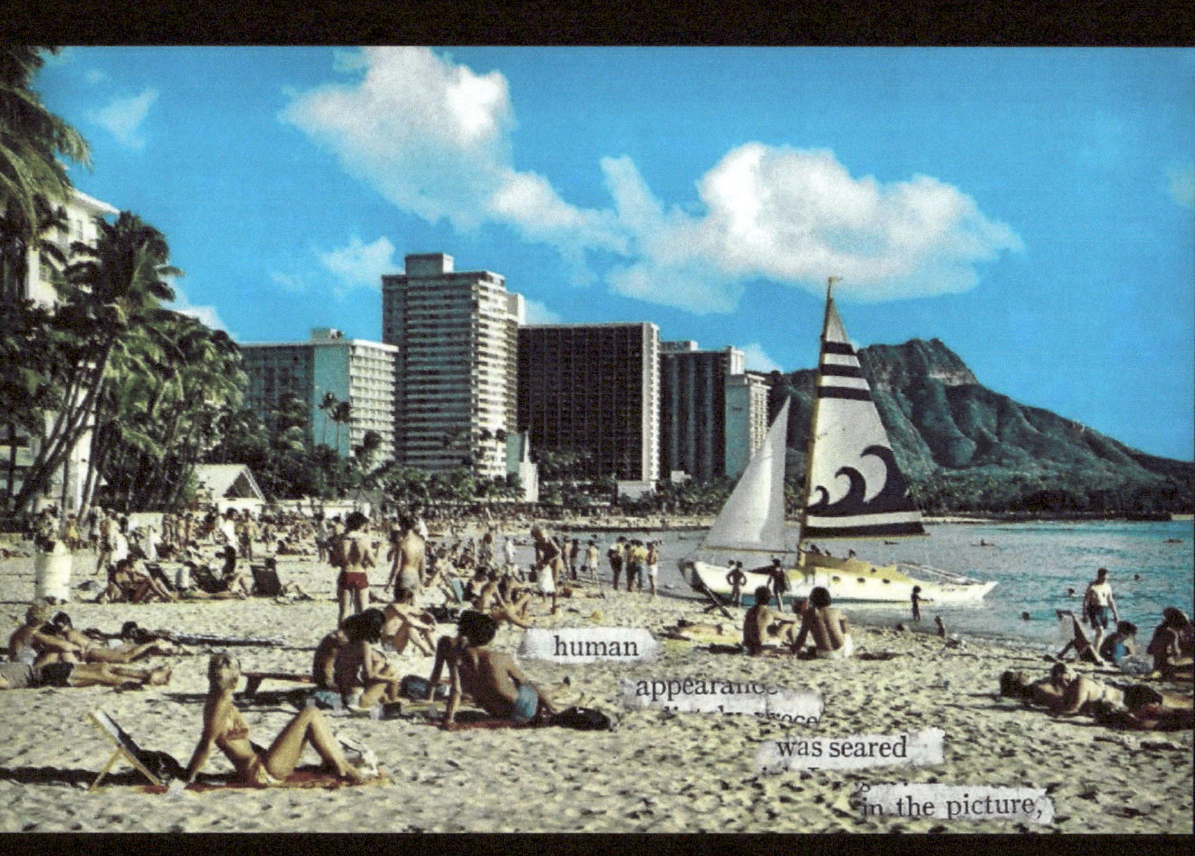
human
appearance
was seared
in the picture,

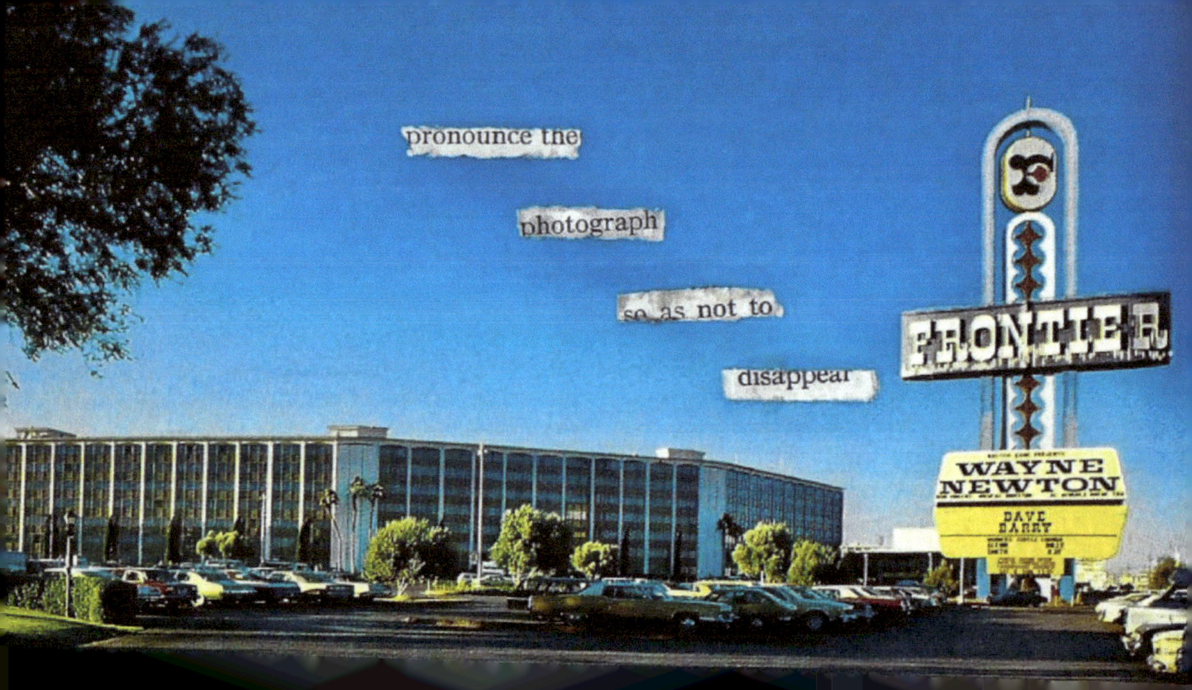

pronounce the
photograph
so as not to
disappear
FRONTIER
WAYNE
NEWTON
DAVE
BARRY

...everything was forgotten

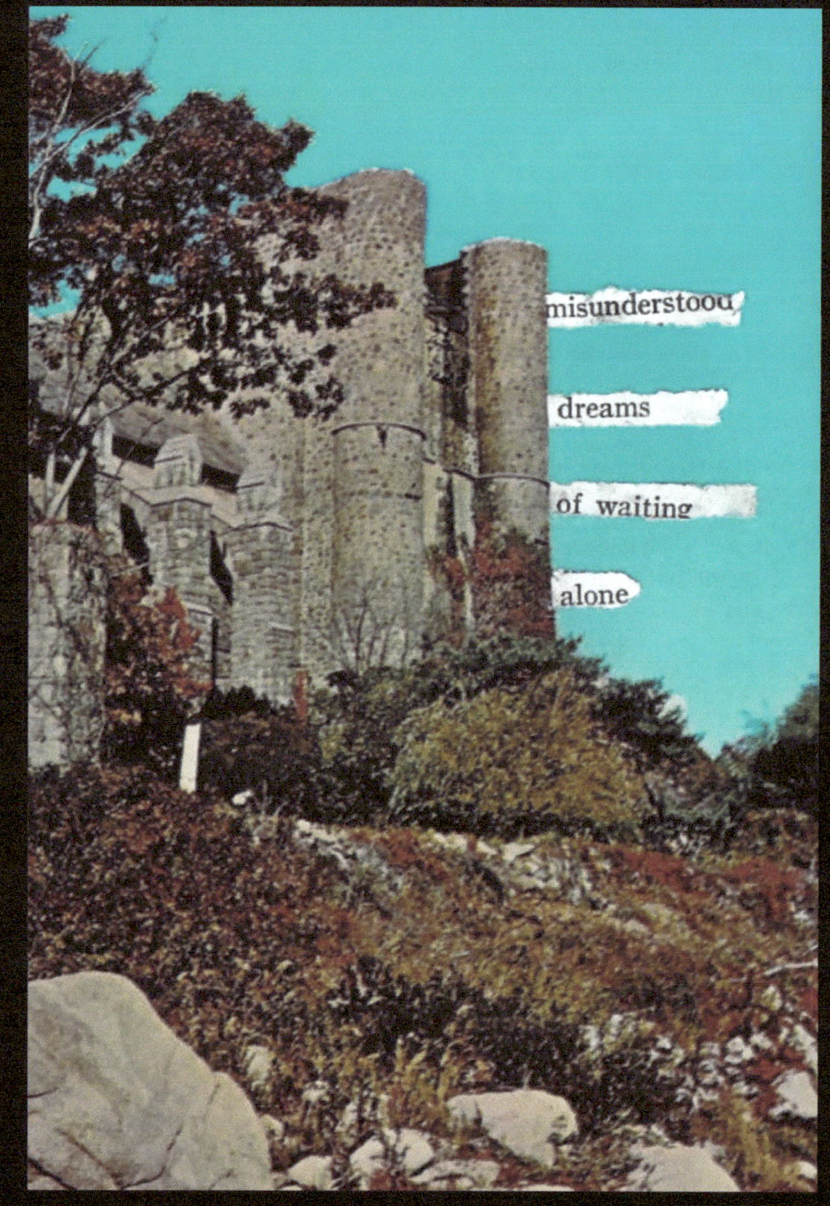
misunderstood
dreams
of waiting
alone

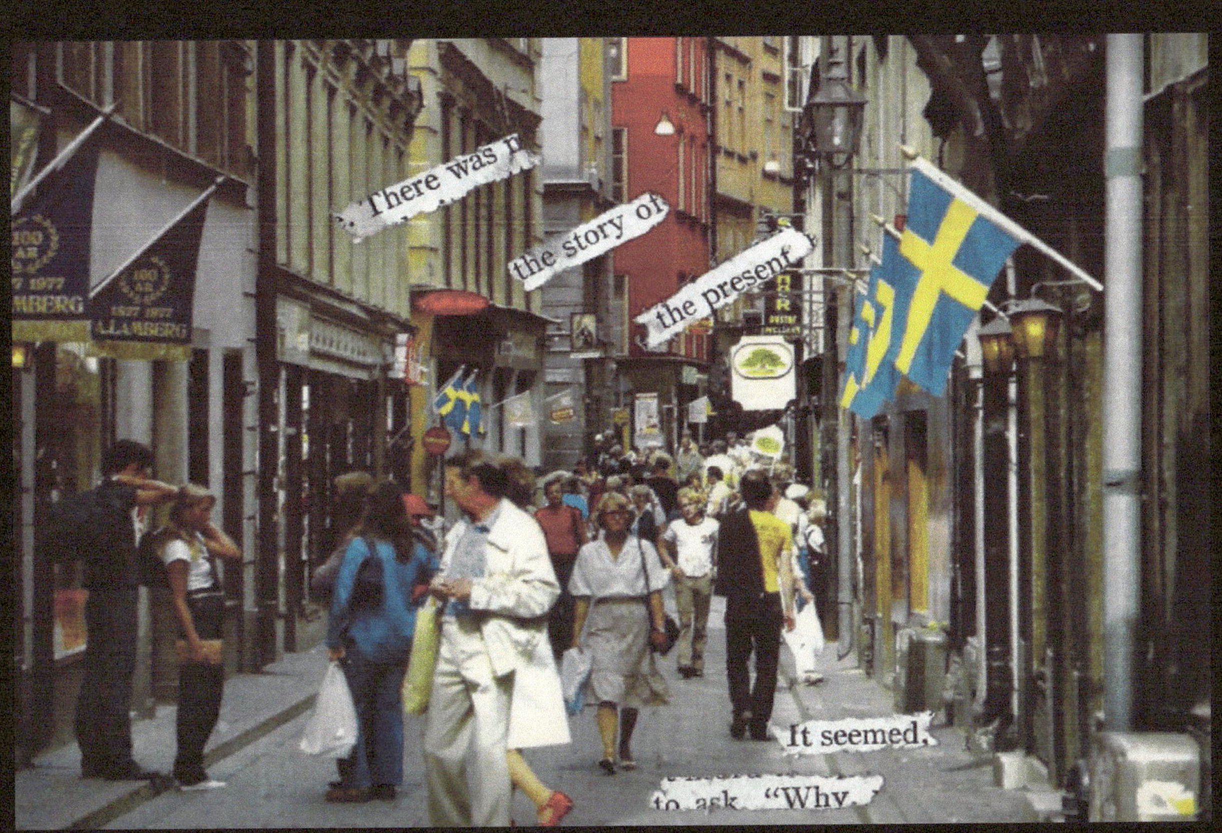
There was
the story of
the present
It seemed,
to ask, "Why

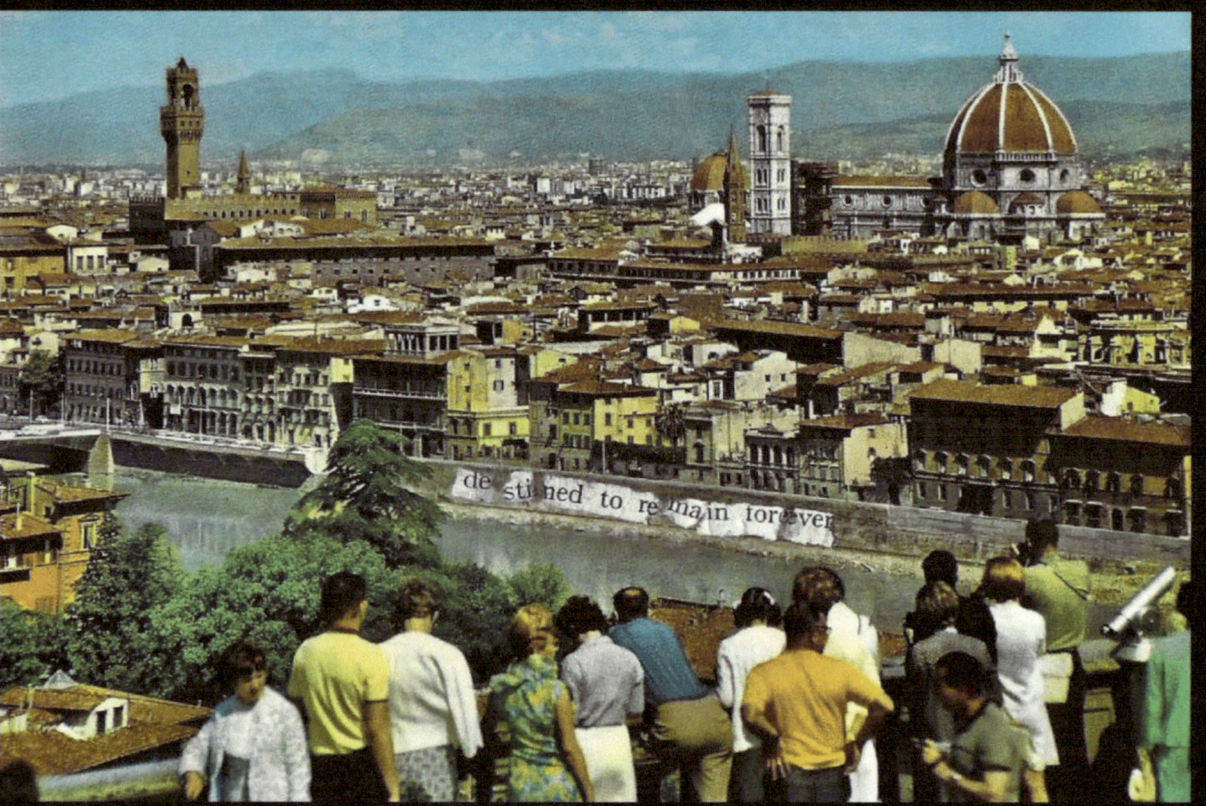
de stined to re main forever

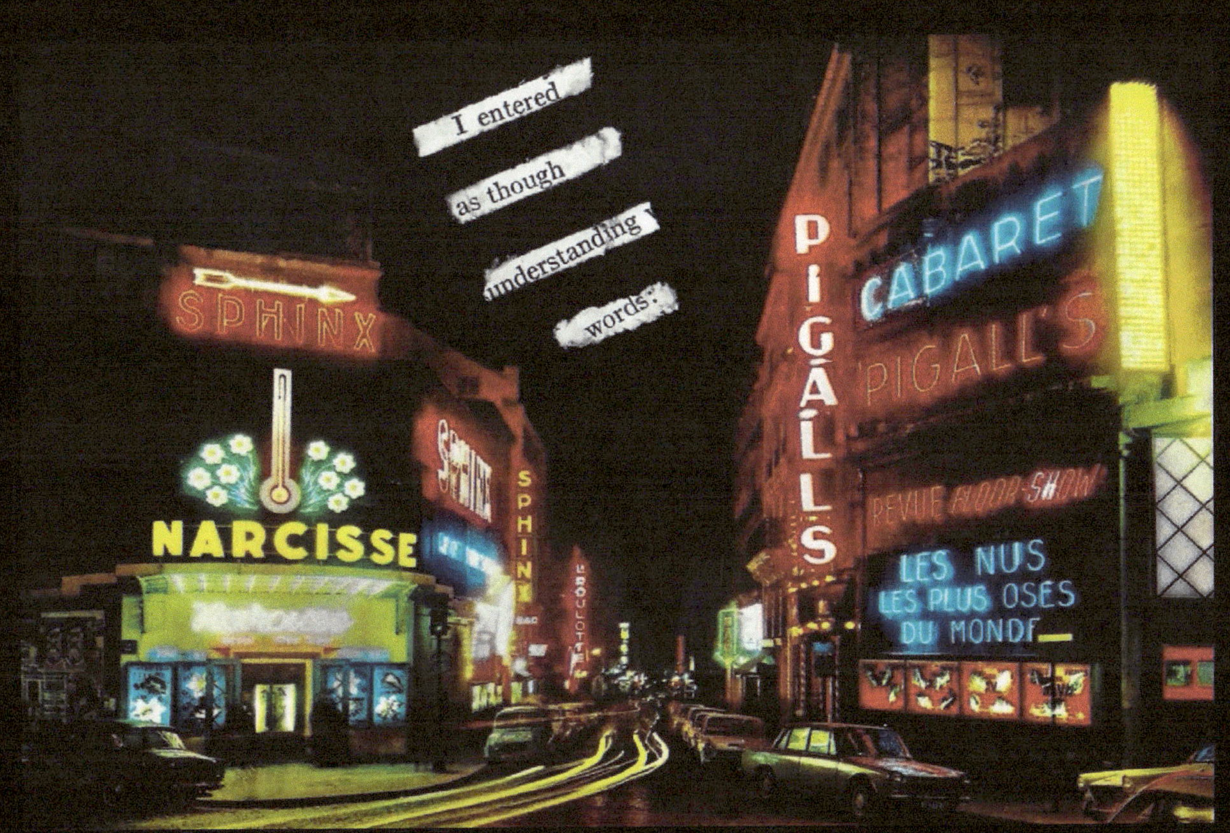
I entered
as though
understanding
words.
SPHINX
NARCISSE
SPHINX
PIGALL'S
CABARET
PIGALL'S
REVUE FLOOR-SHOW
LES NUS
LES PLUS OSES
DU MONDE

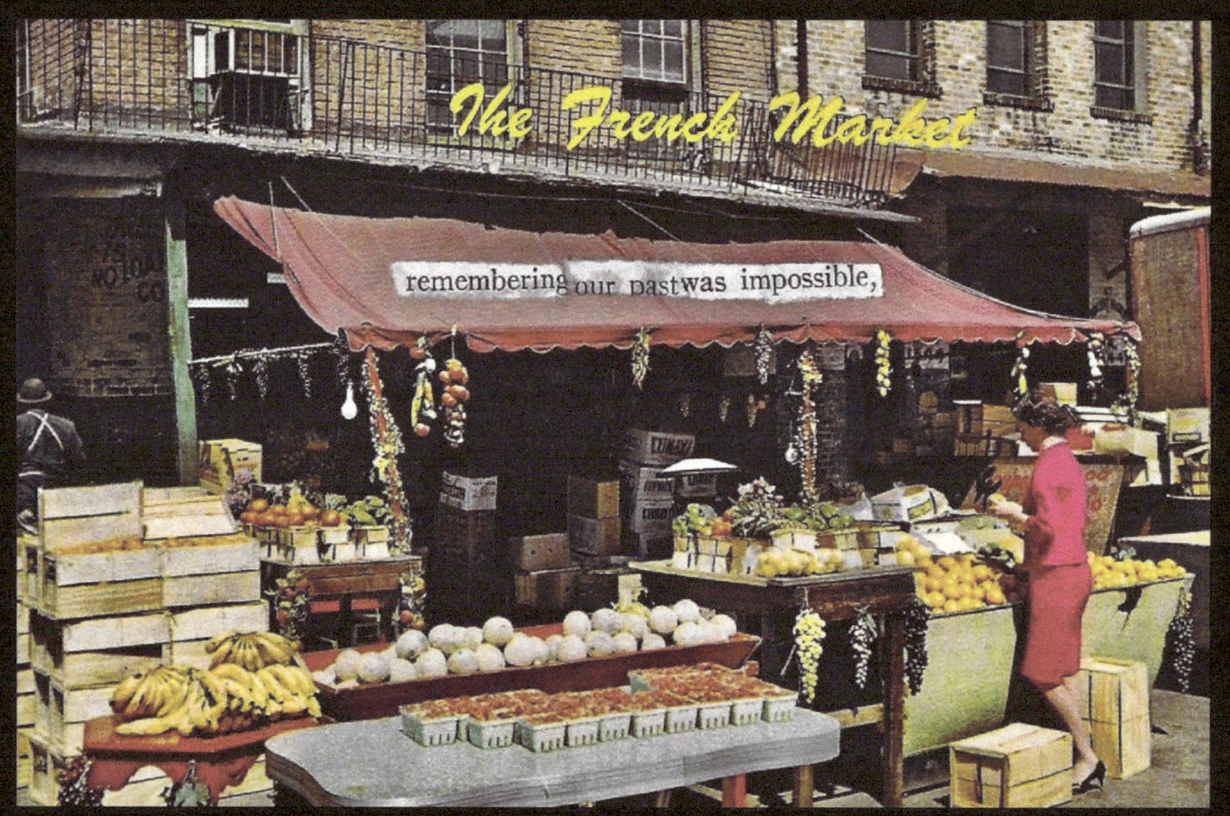
The French Market
remembering our past was impossible,

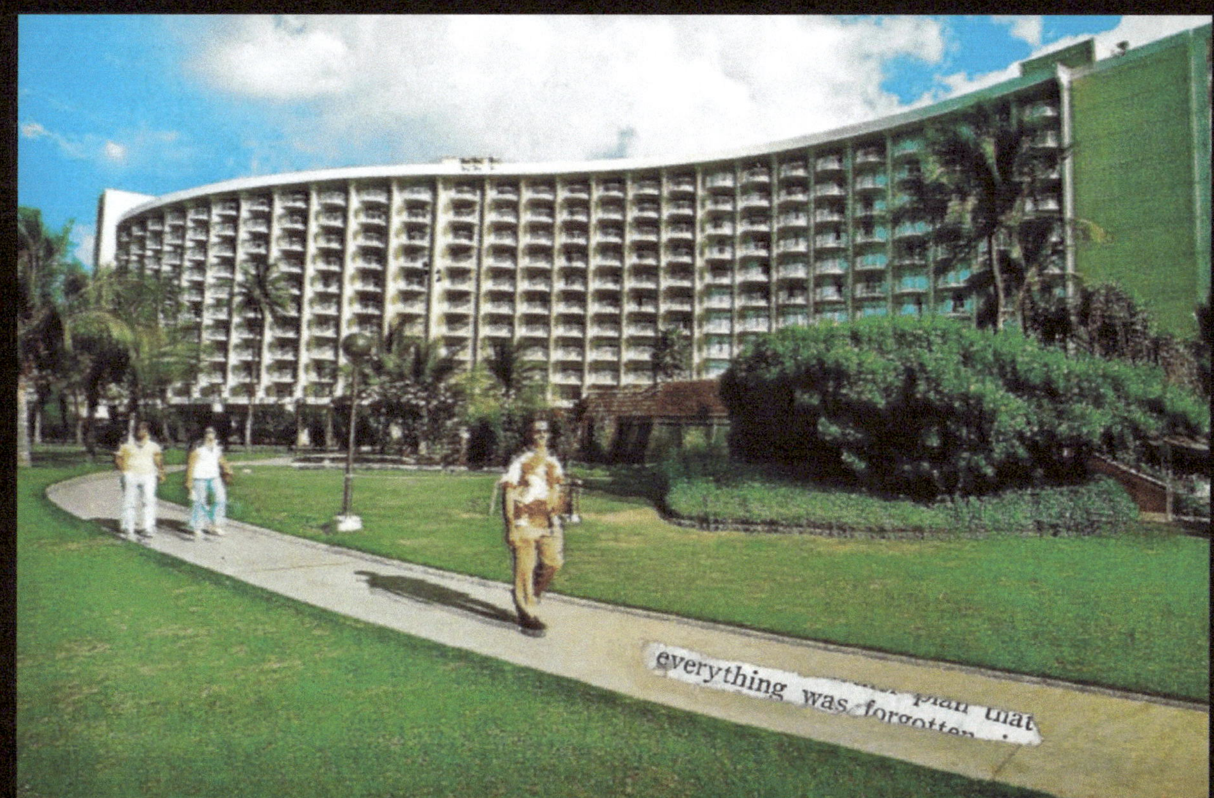
everything was forgotten
plan that

...between the end,

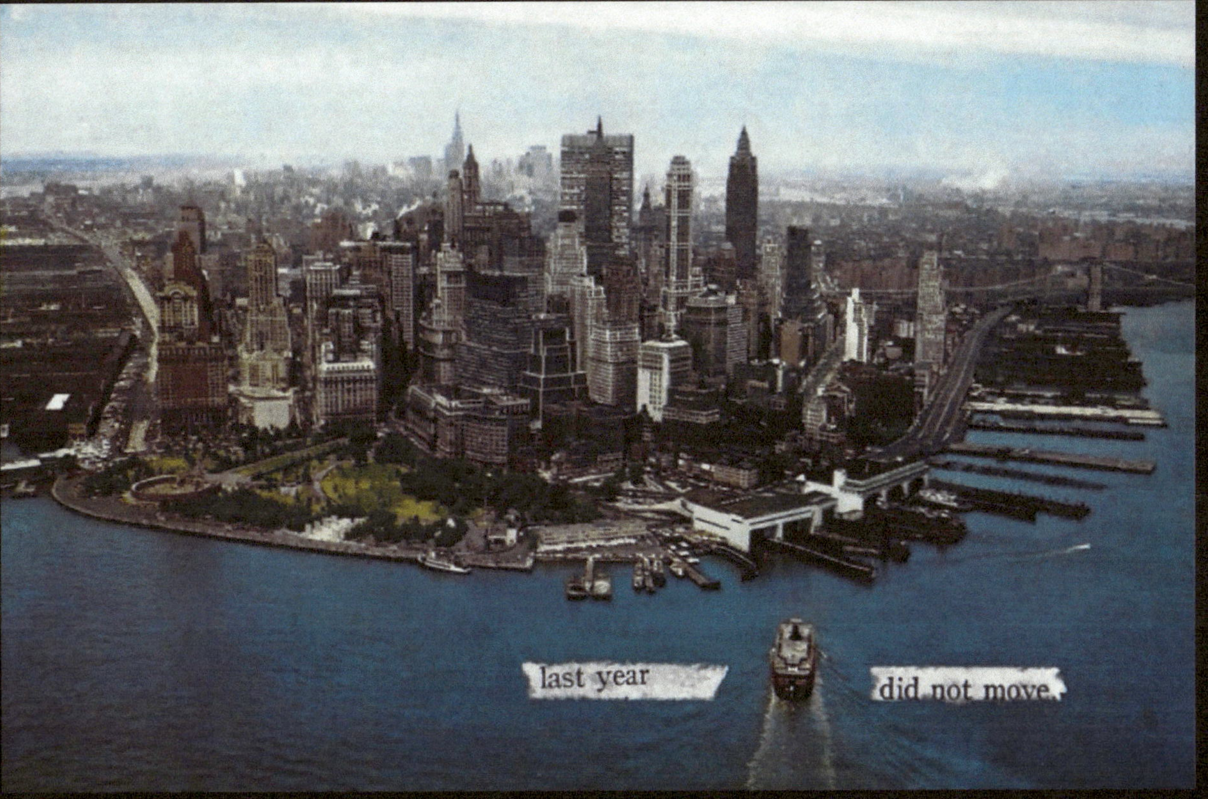

last year
did not move.

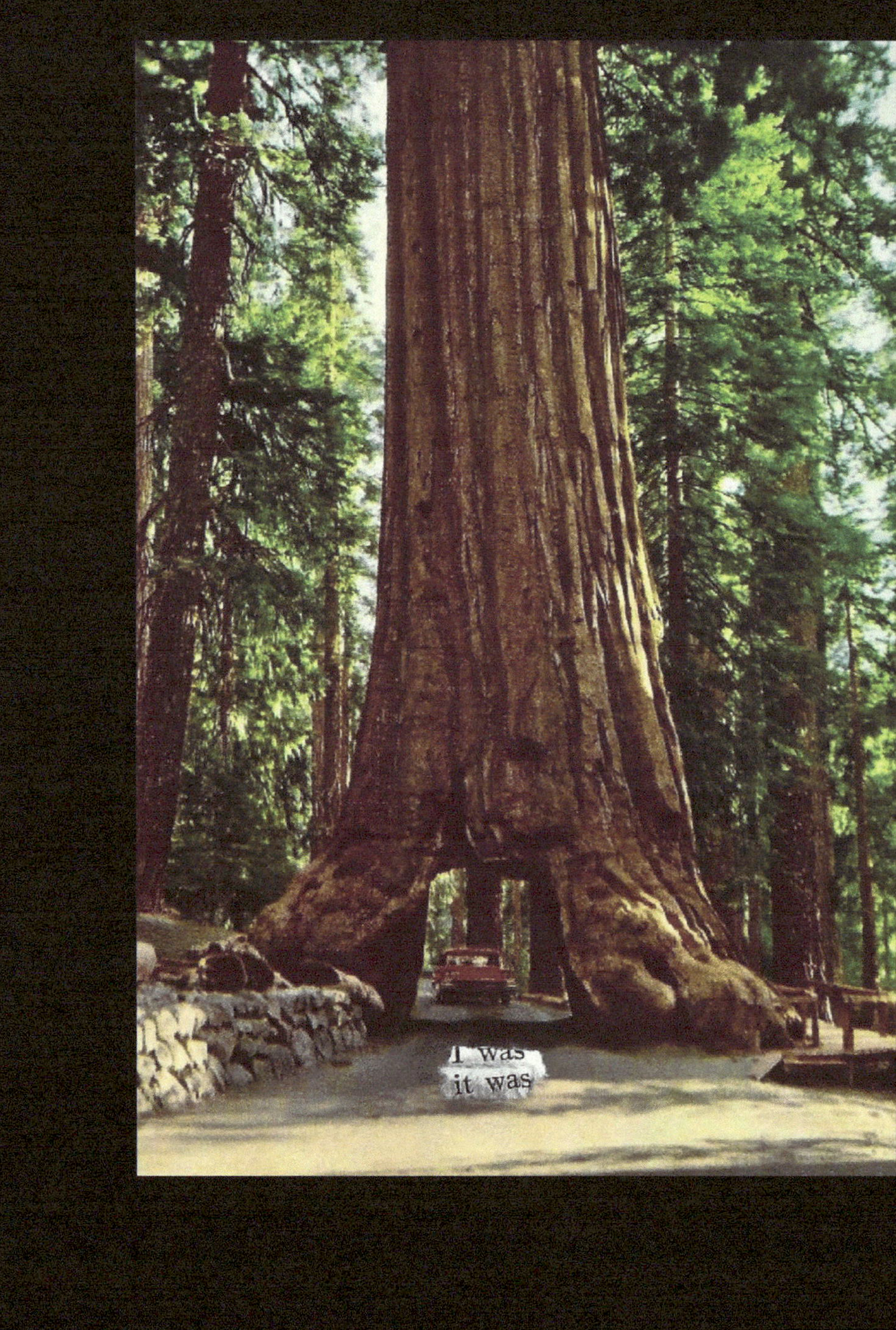
I was
it was

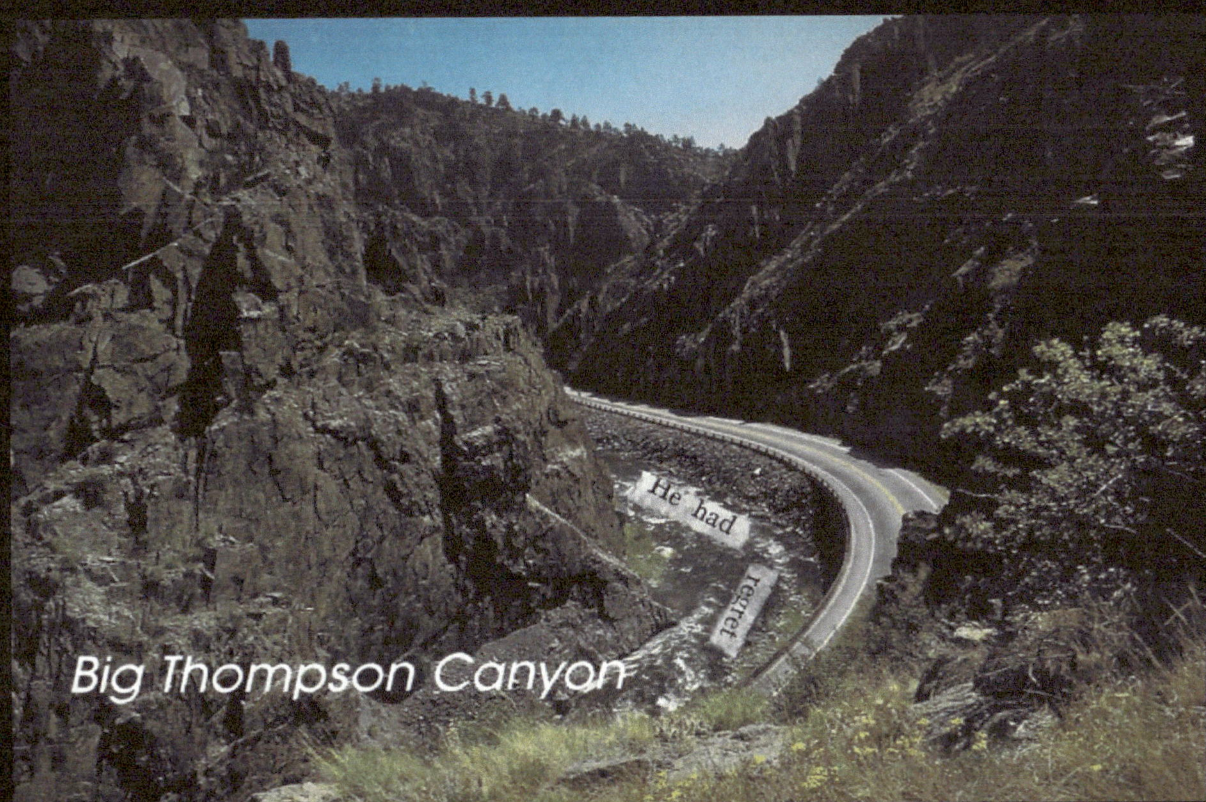
He had
regret
Big Thompson Canyon

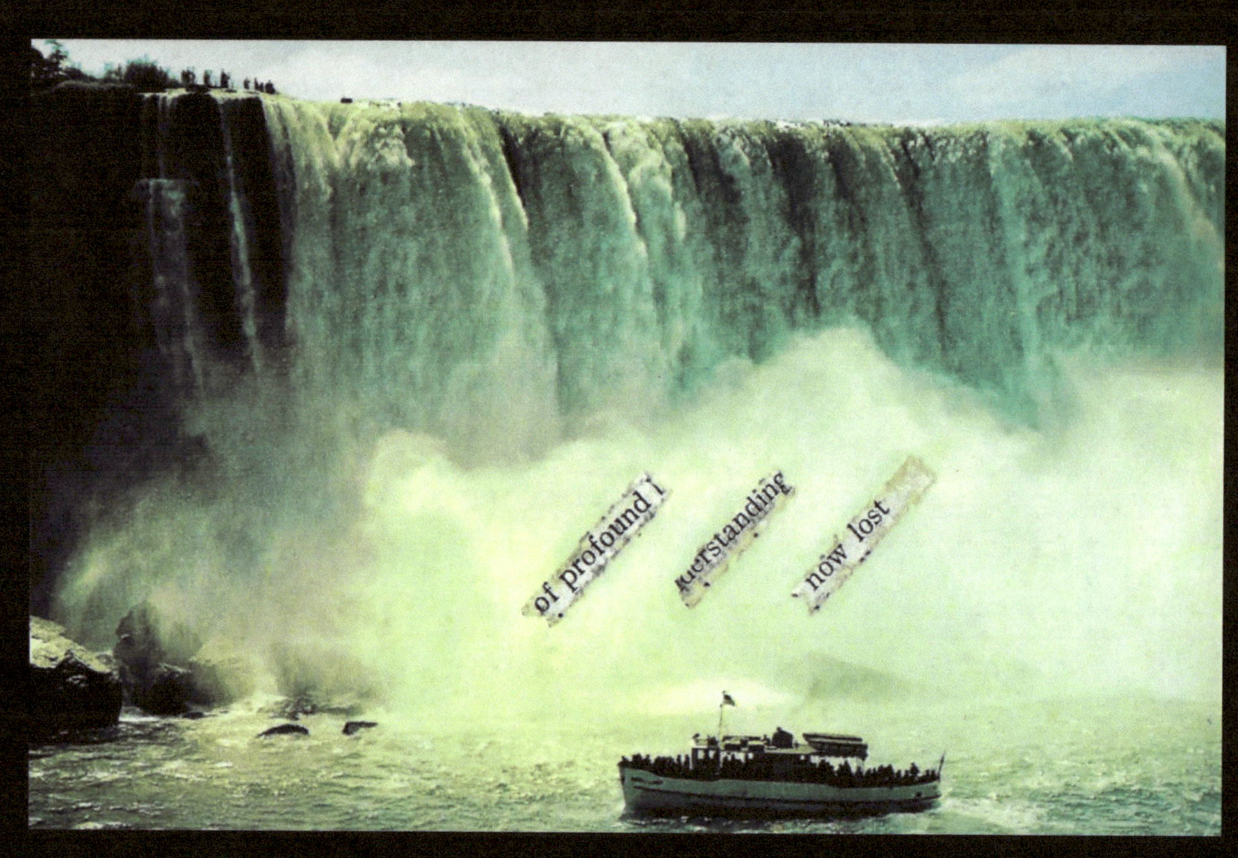
of profound
uerstanding
now lost

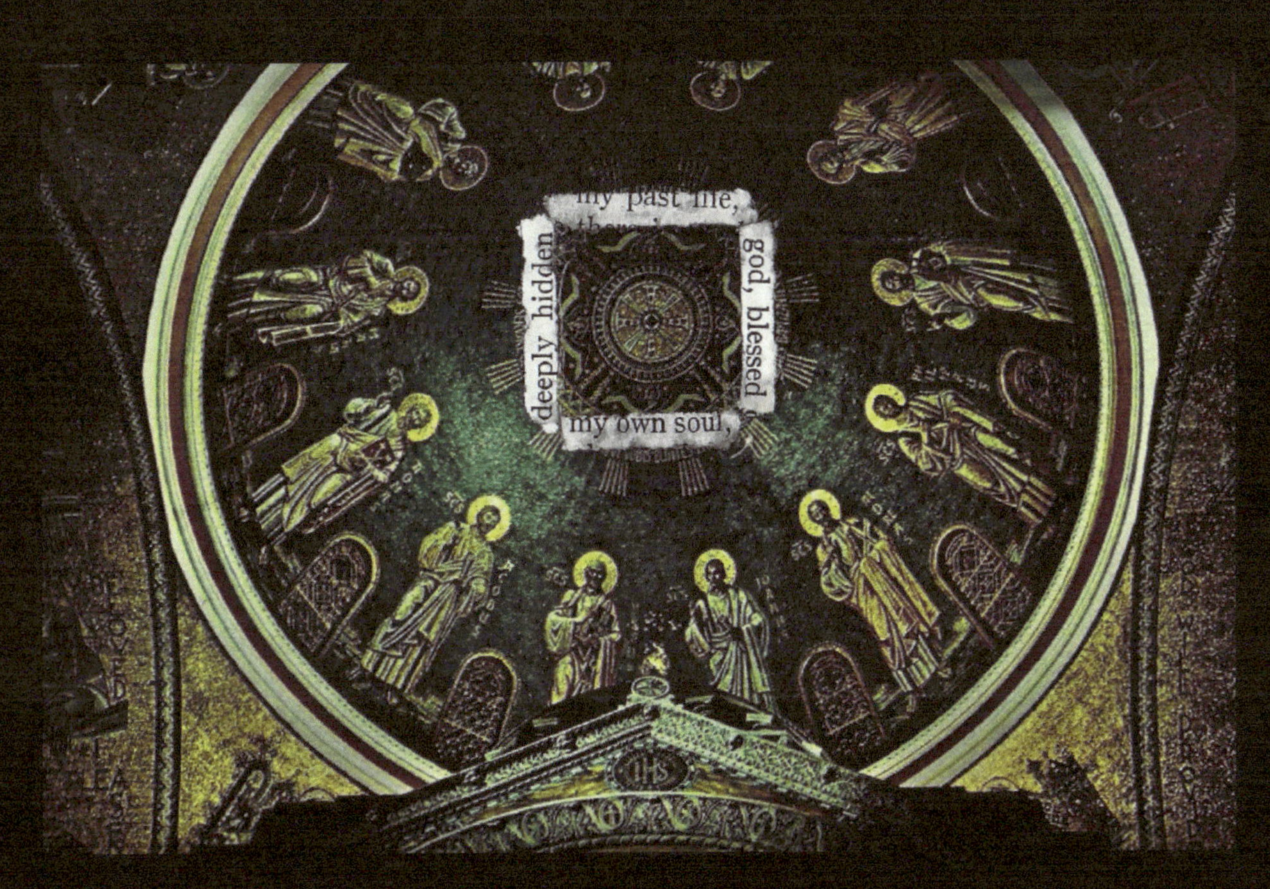
my past life,
deeply hidden
god, blessed
my own soul,

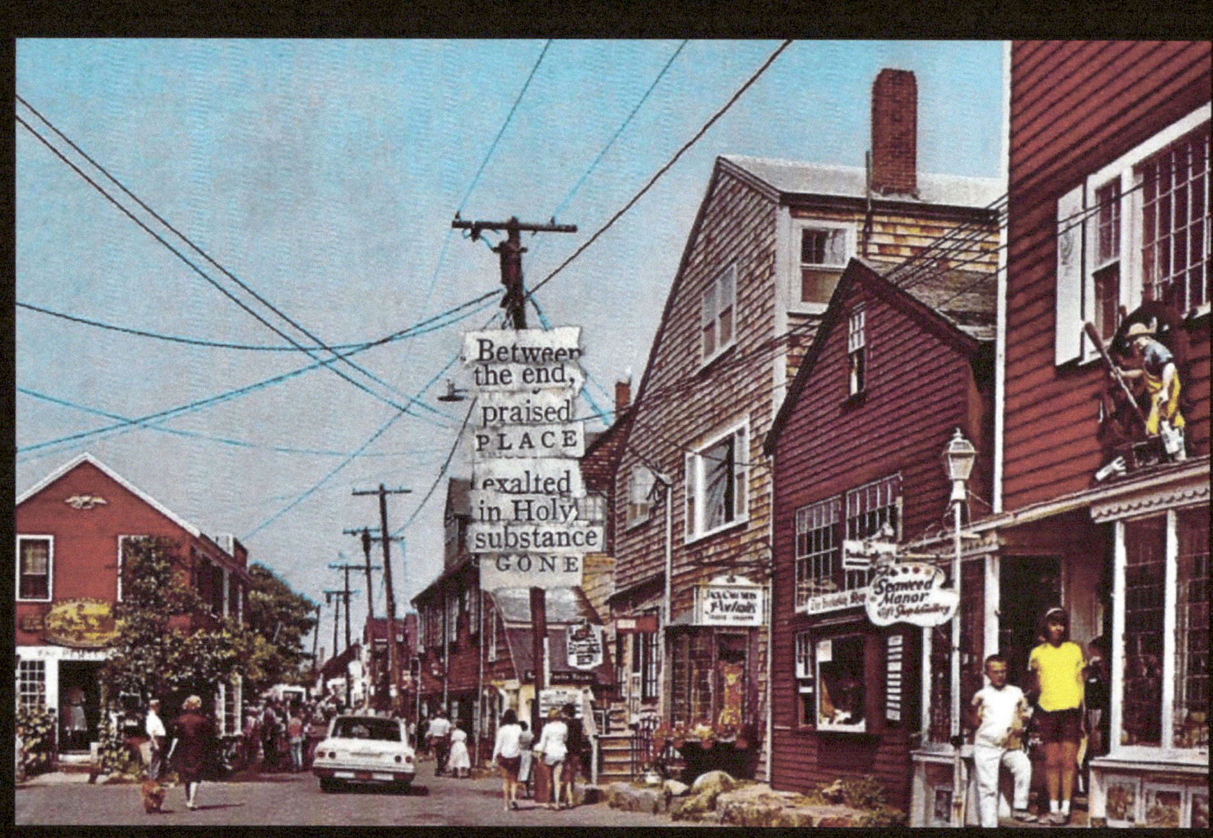
Between
the end,
praised
PLACE
exalted
in Holy
substance
GONE

...poetry of my failure

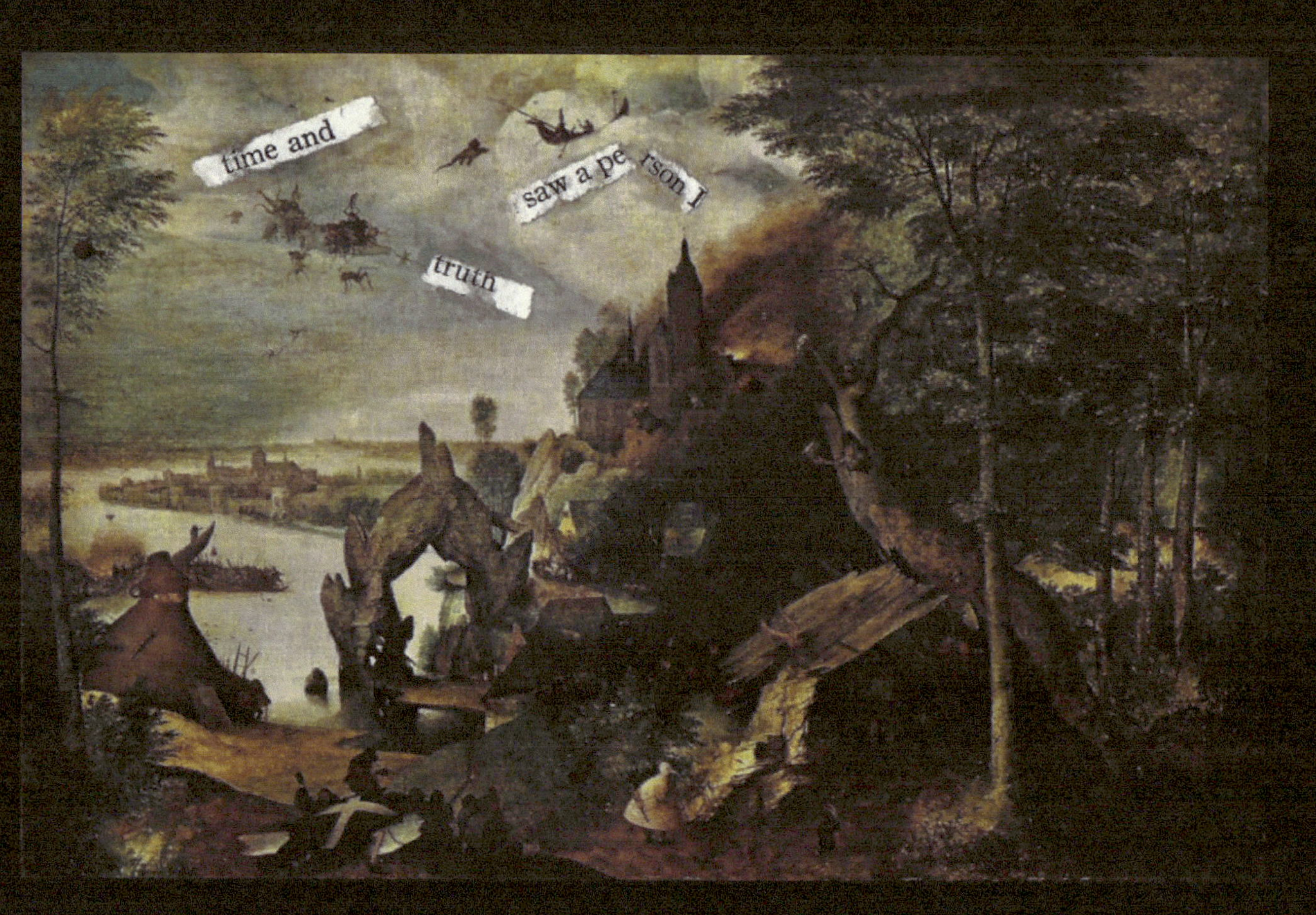

time and
saw a pe rson I
truth

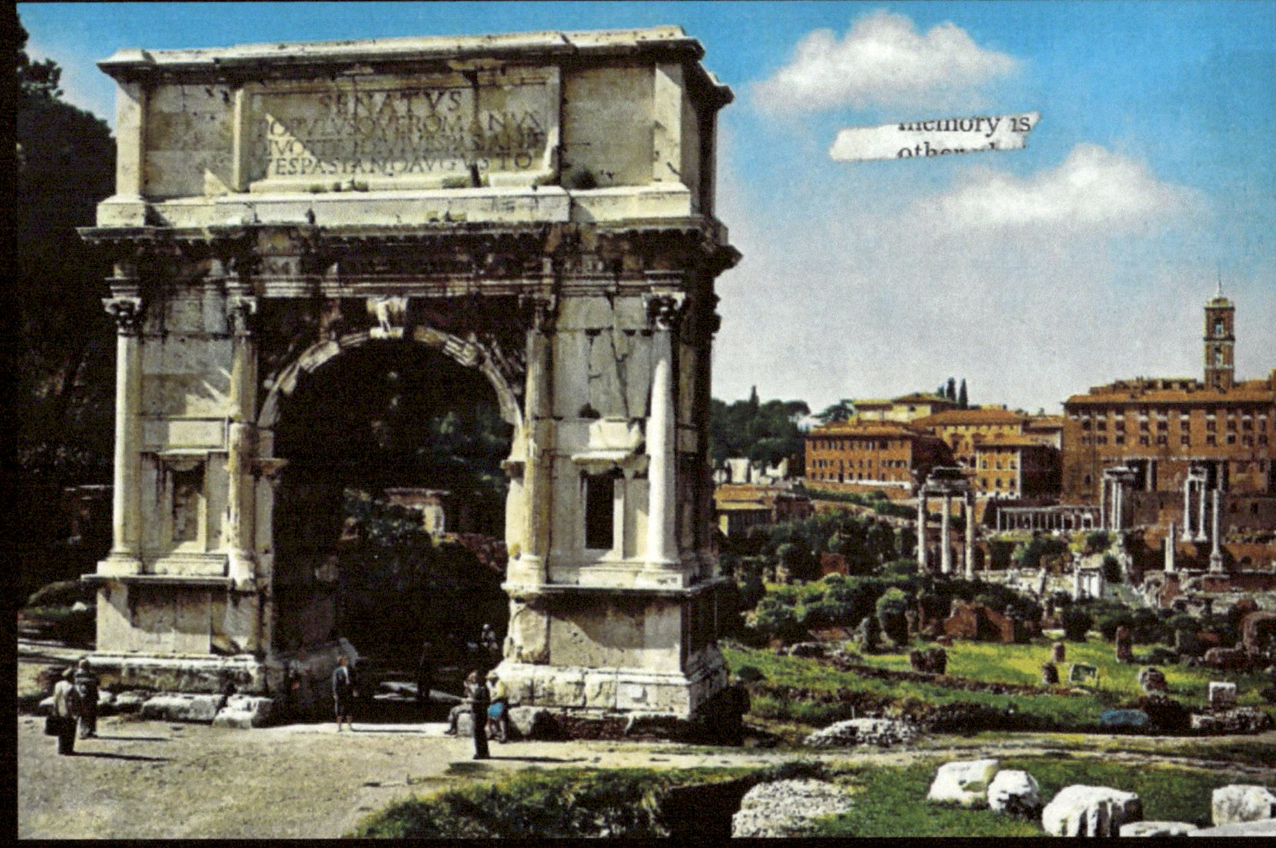
memory is
other

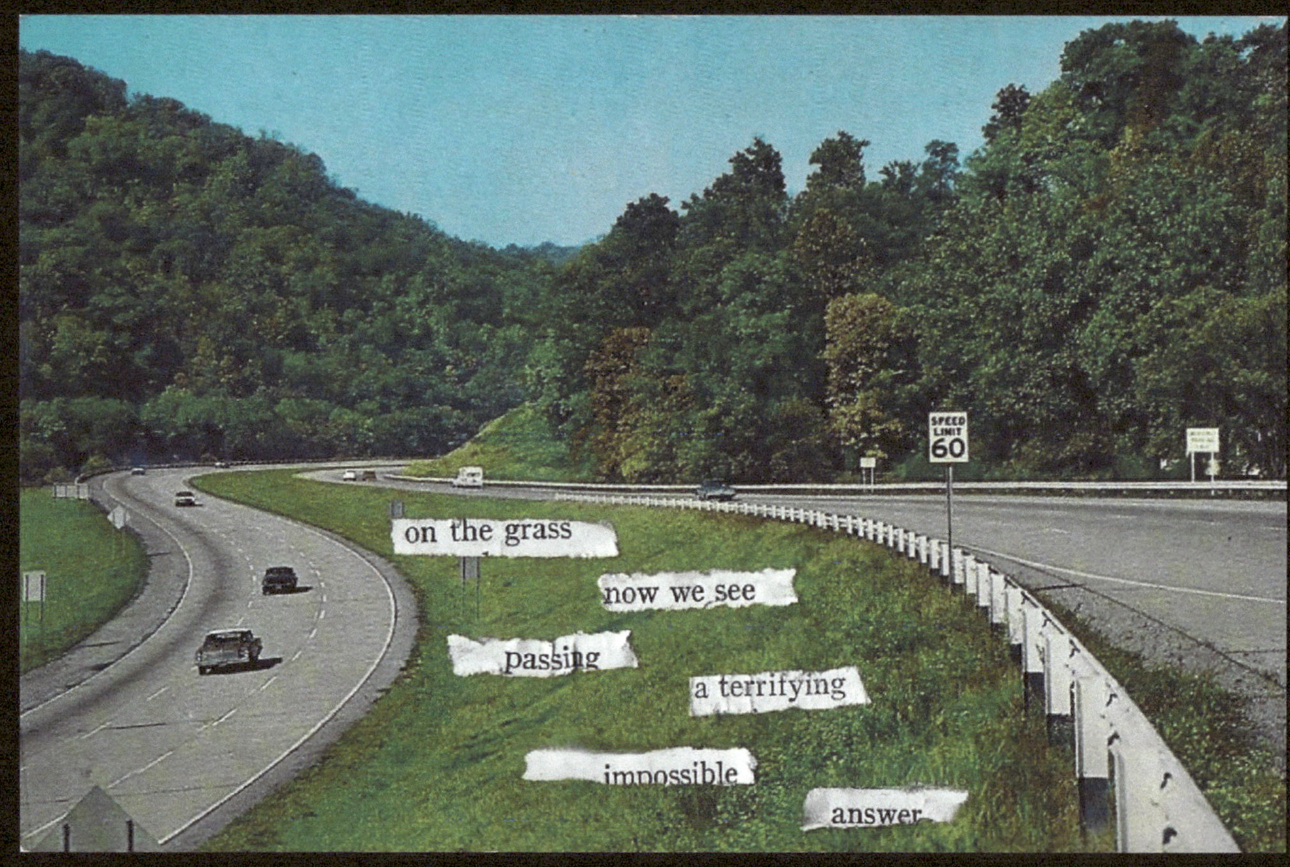

on the grass
now we see
passing
a terrifying
impossible
answer
SPEED LIMIT 60

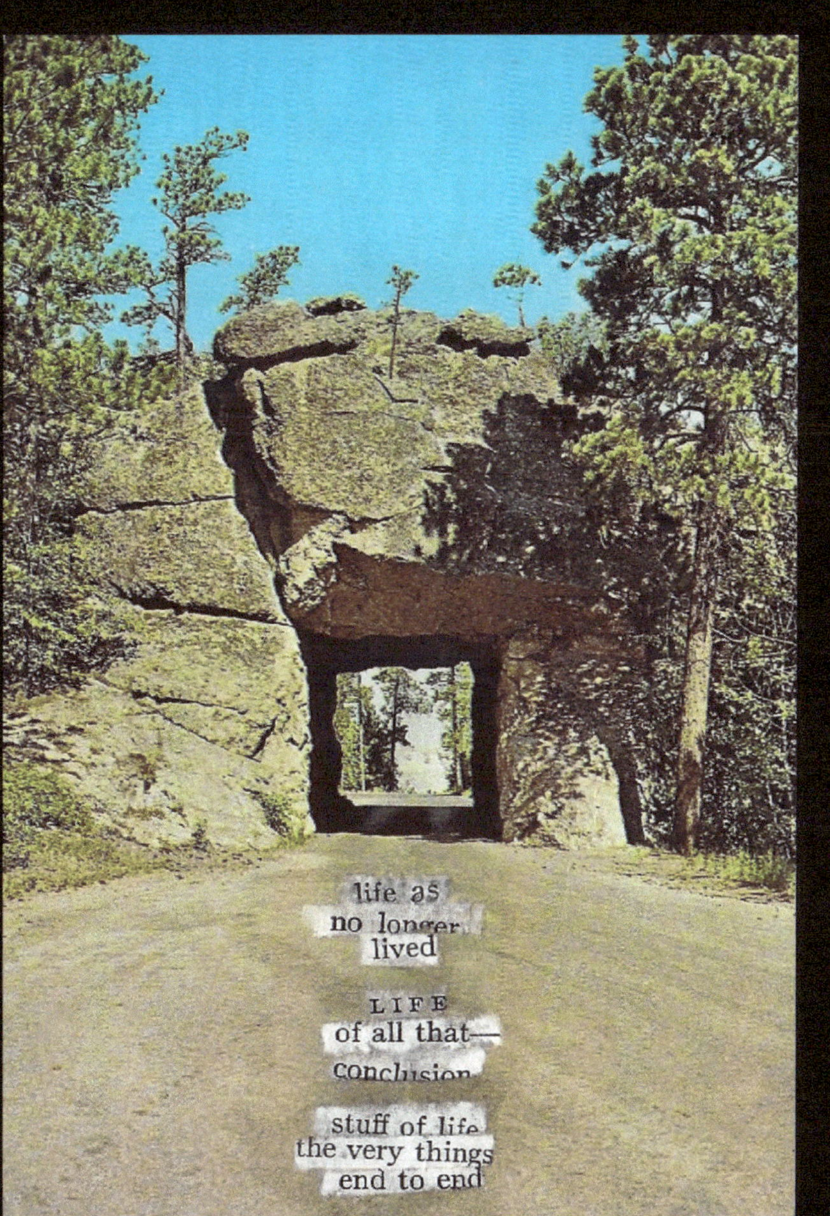

life as
no longer
lived

LIFE
of all that—

conclusion

stuff of life
the very things
end to end

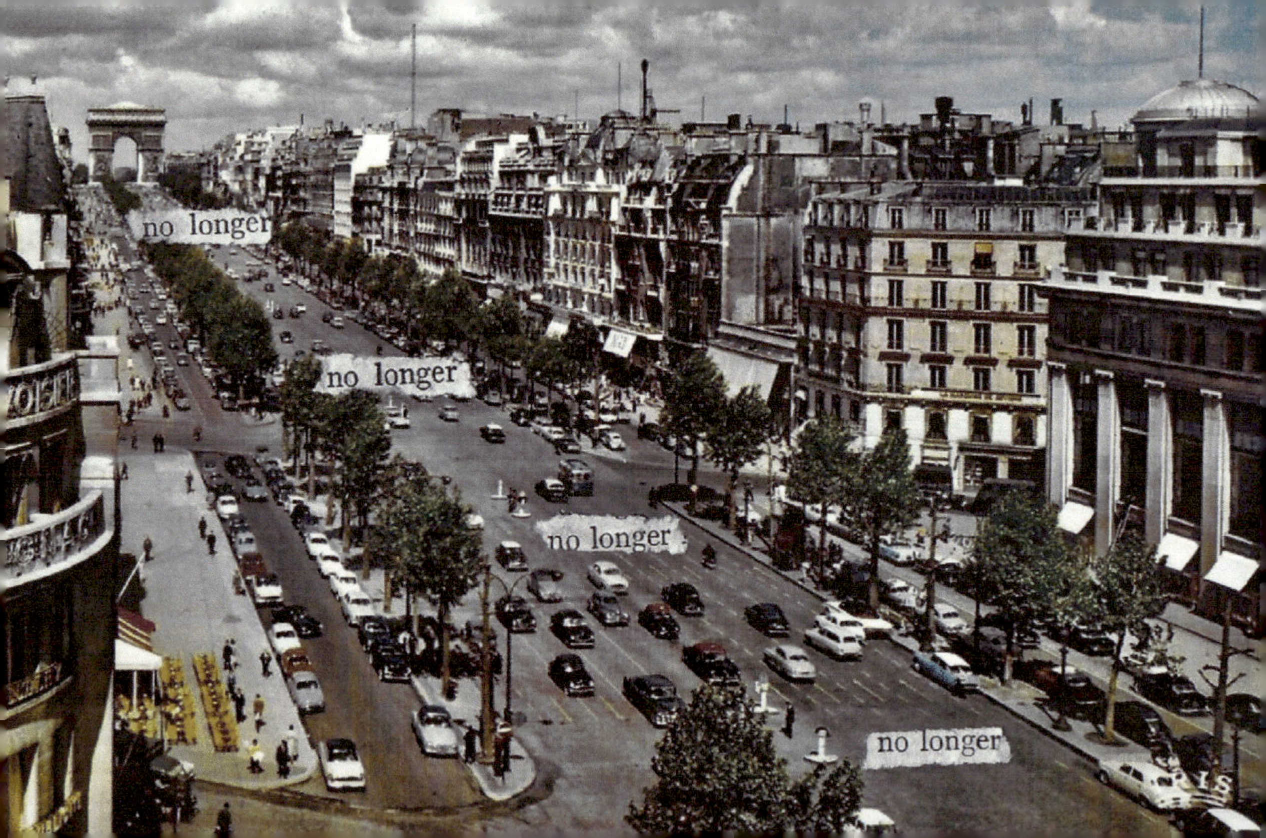

no longer
no longer
no longer
no longer

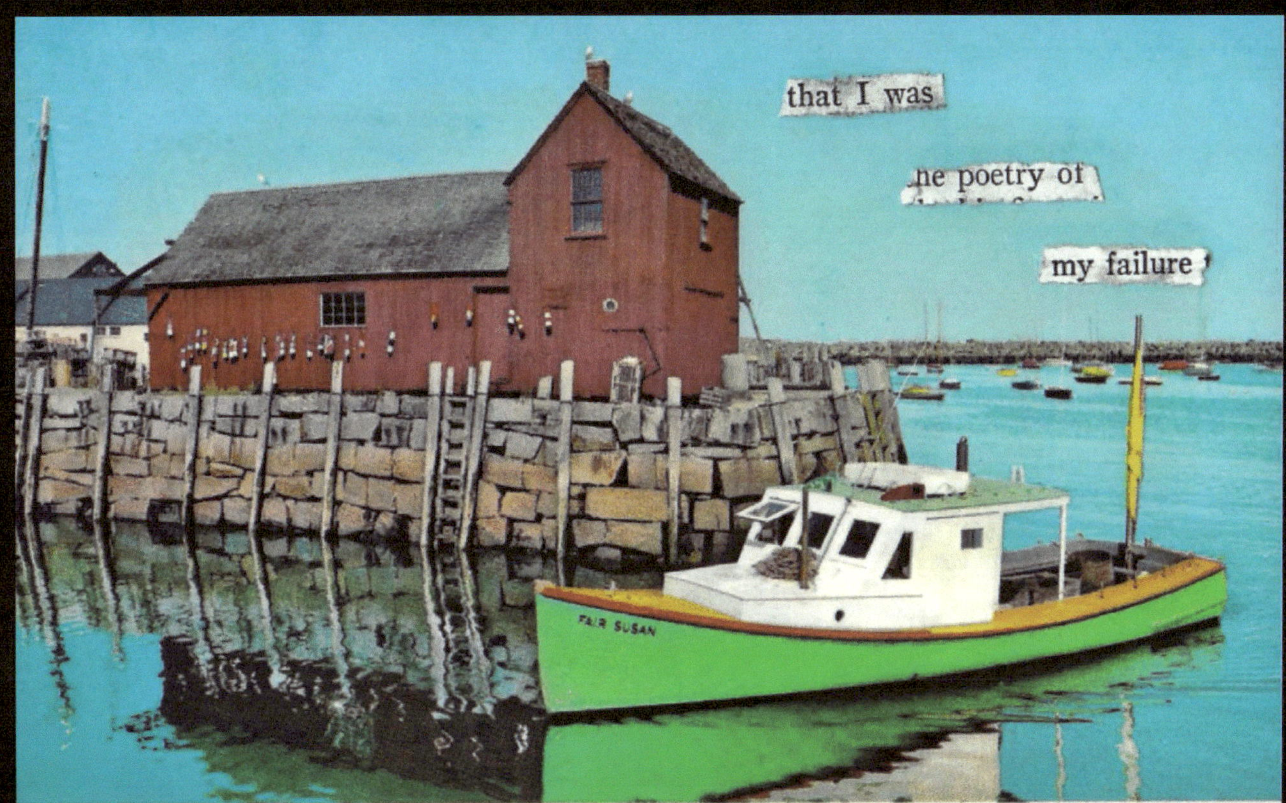

Famous Motif Number One, Rockport, Mass.

...was not, after all

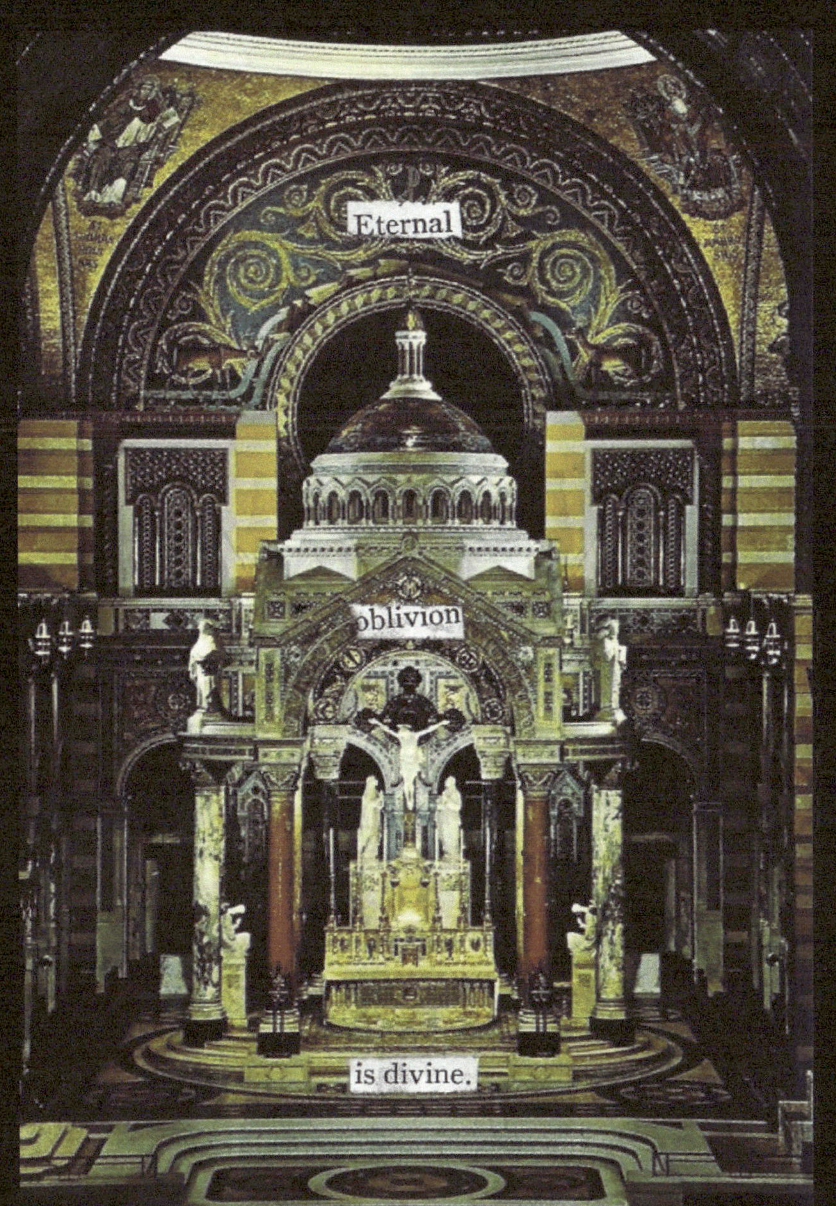
Eternal
oblivion
is divine.

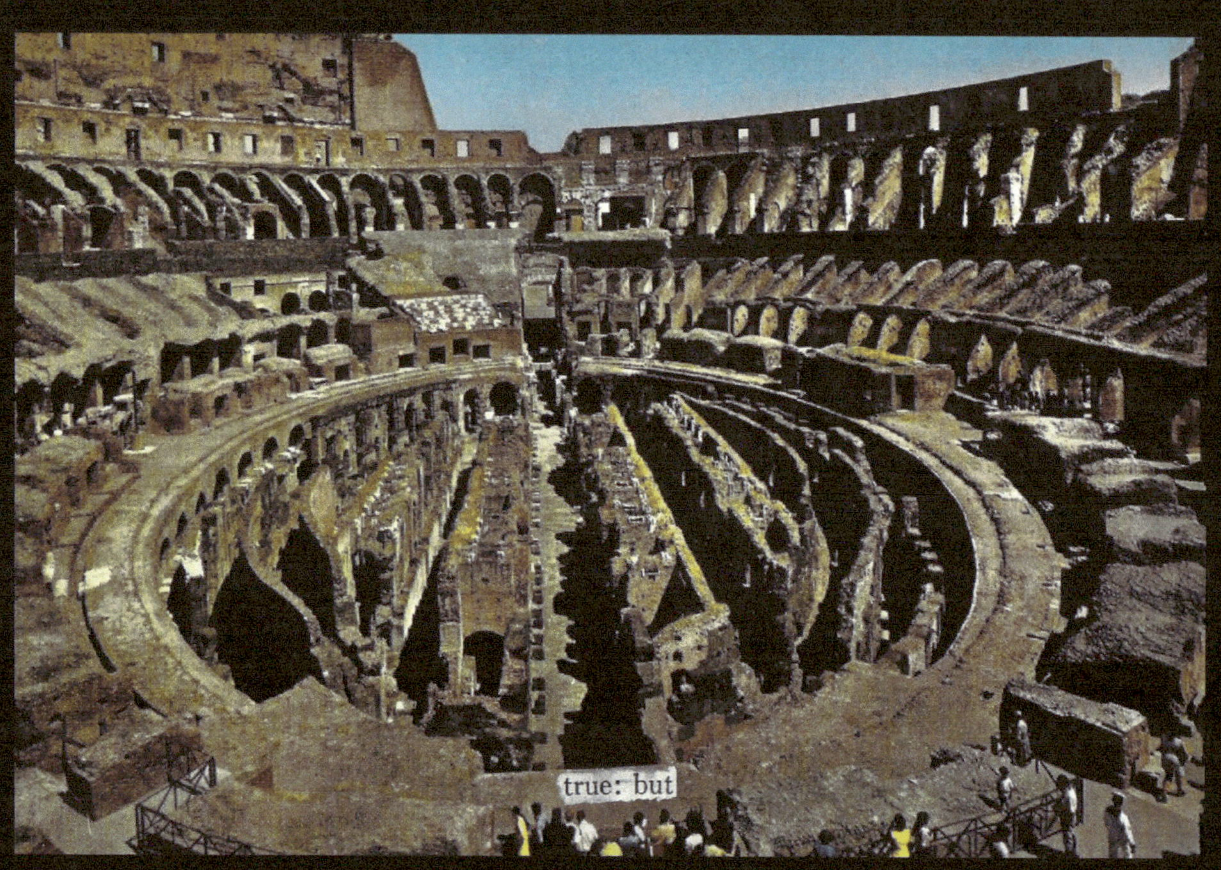
true: but

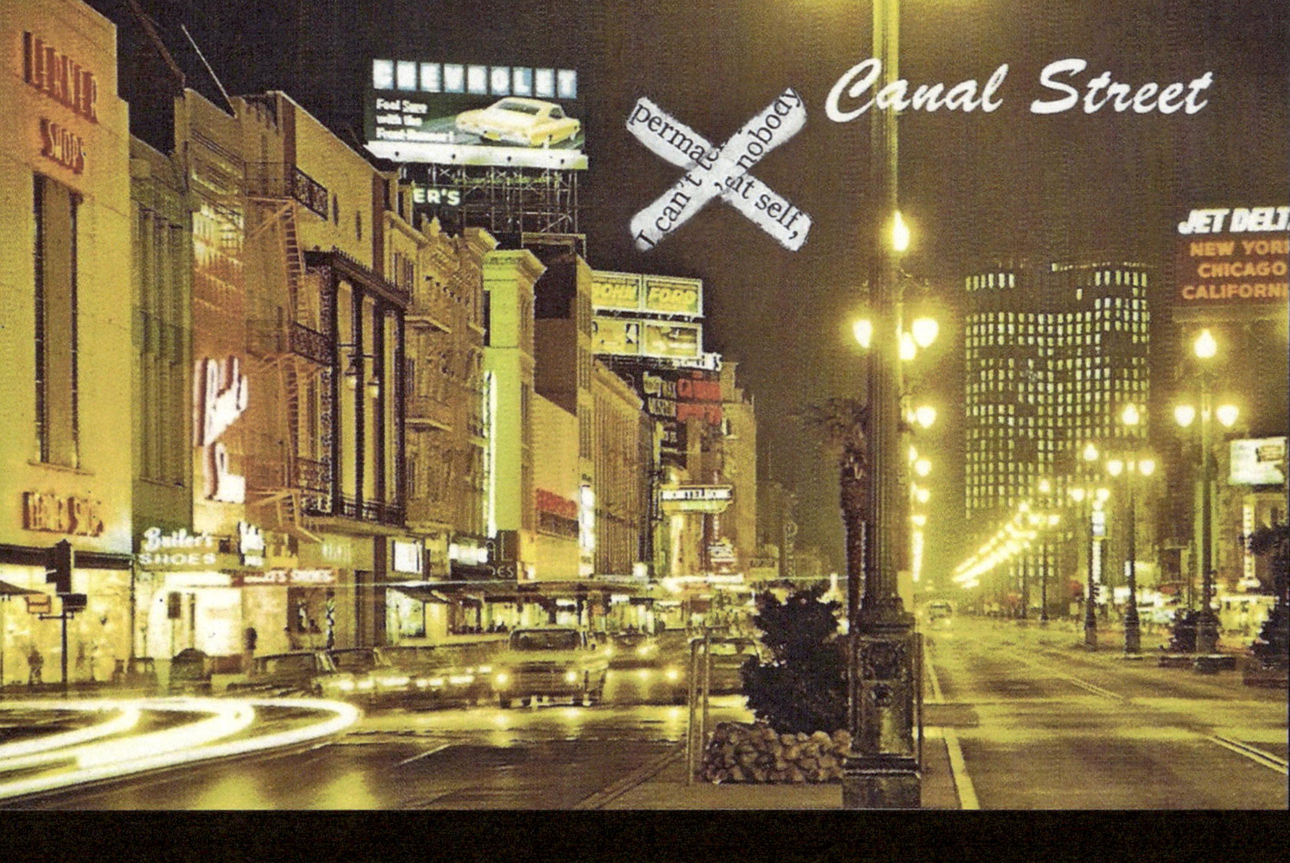

CHEVROLET
Feel Sure
with the
Front Runner!
LEADER
SHOPS
ER'S
BOYD FORD
Butler's
SHOES
HES
Canal Street
permac
nobody
I can't
at self,
JET DELT
NEW YOR
CHICAGO
CALIFORNI

after,
to say
mind
in love
thinking
other
see
still
word
my body
still
suffer
time to be
now,
immediat
murmur,
to read!
past whole
between
memory
fail to
who not,
enough
world,
But ved
listen
so long
names
so far
feelin
death
time
is not
tracing
room
read
hear
world
window,
whole
far who
I think
word
I had
absence

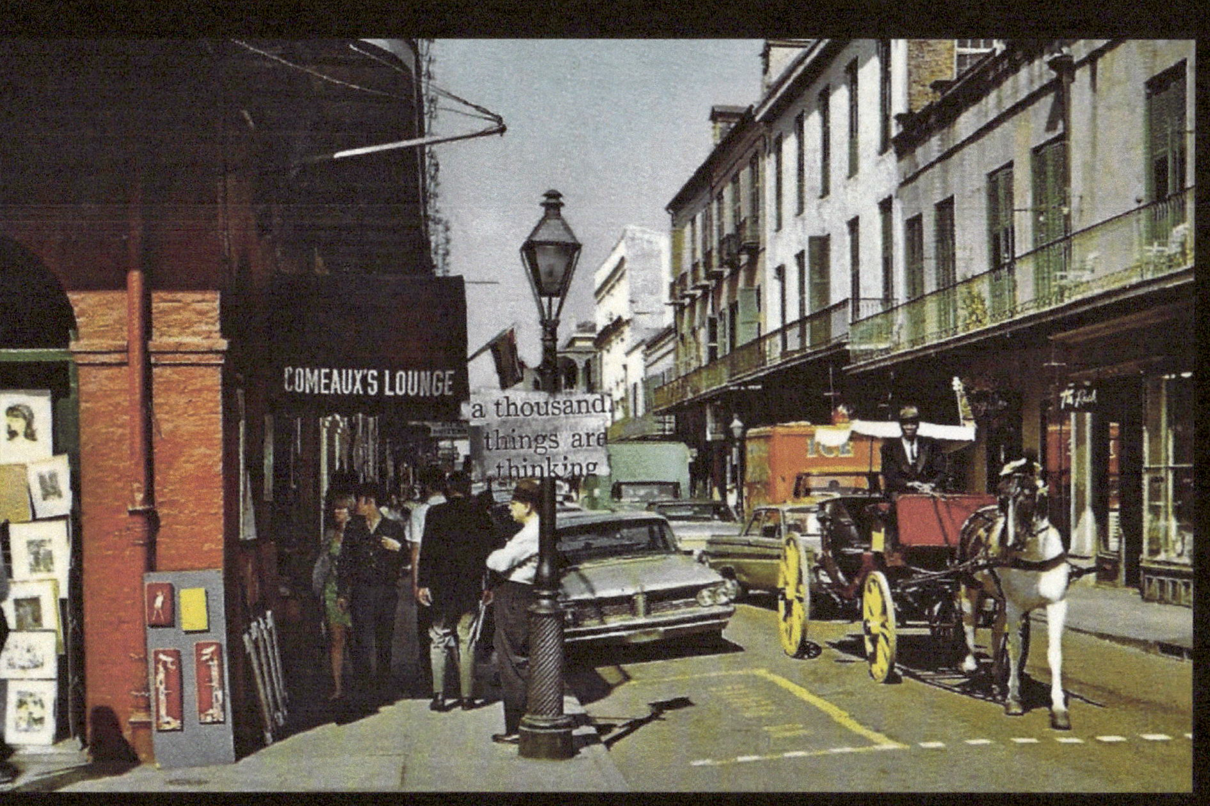
COMEAUX'S LOUNGE
a thousand
things are
thinking

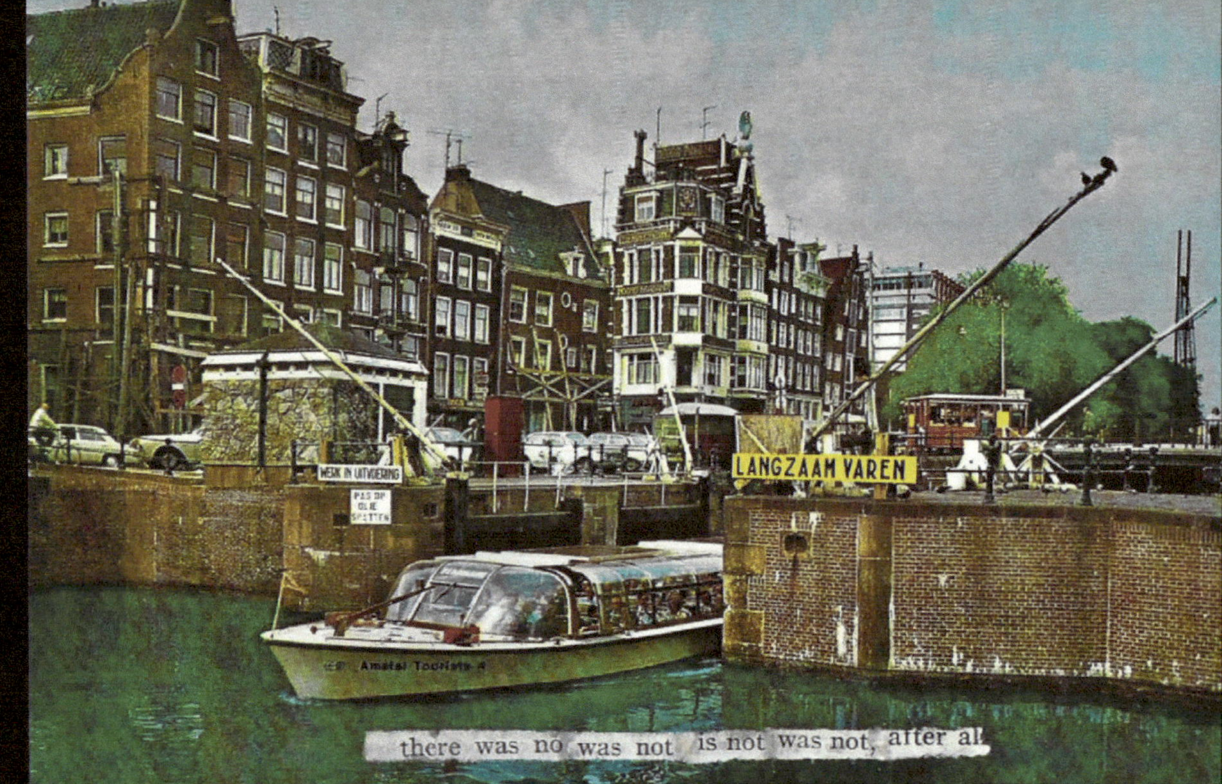

there was no was not is not was not, after all

...glimpse of time, memory of place

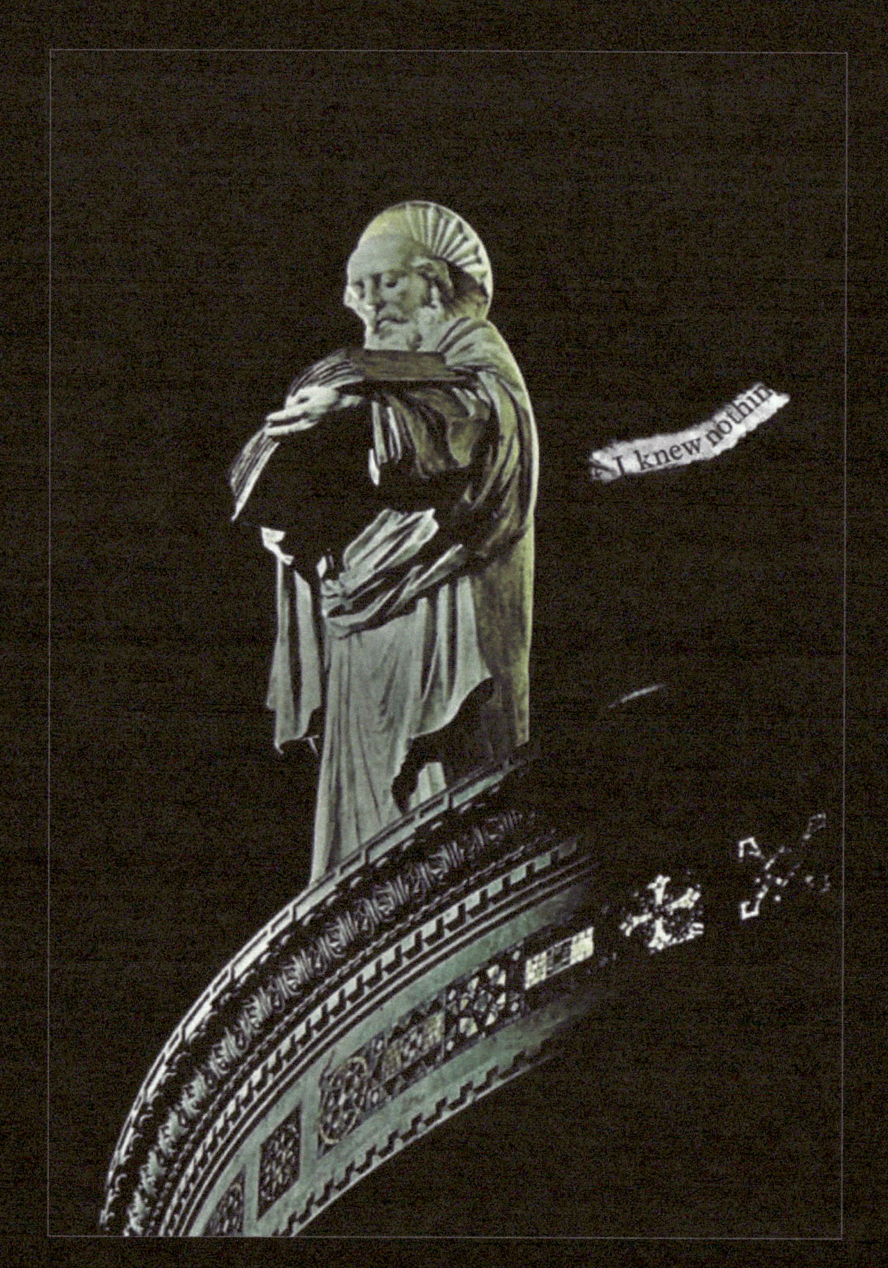

I knew nothin

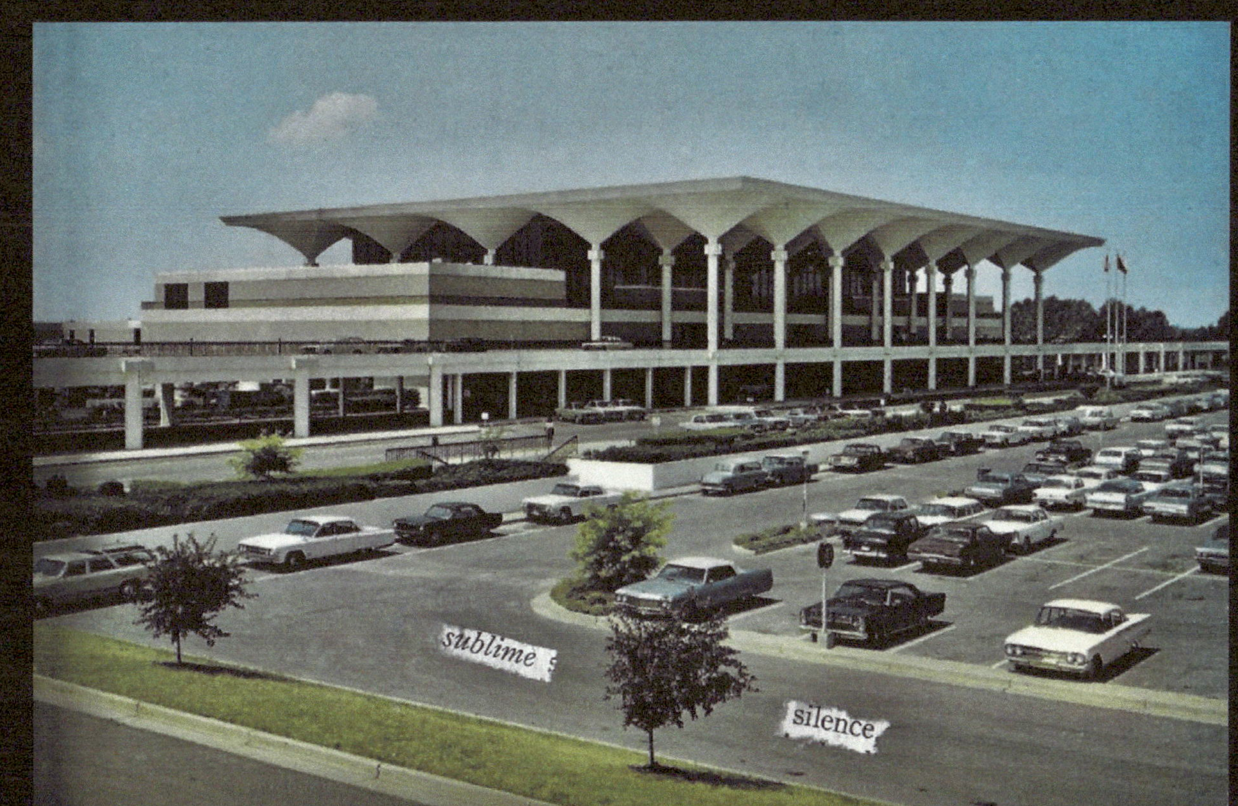

sublime
silence

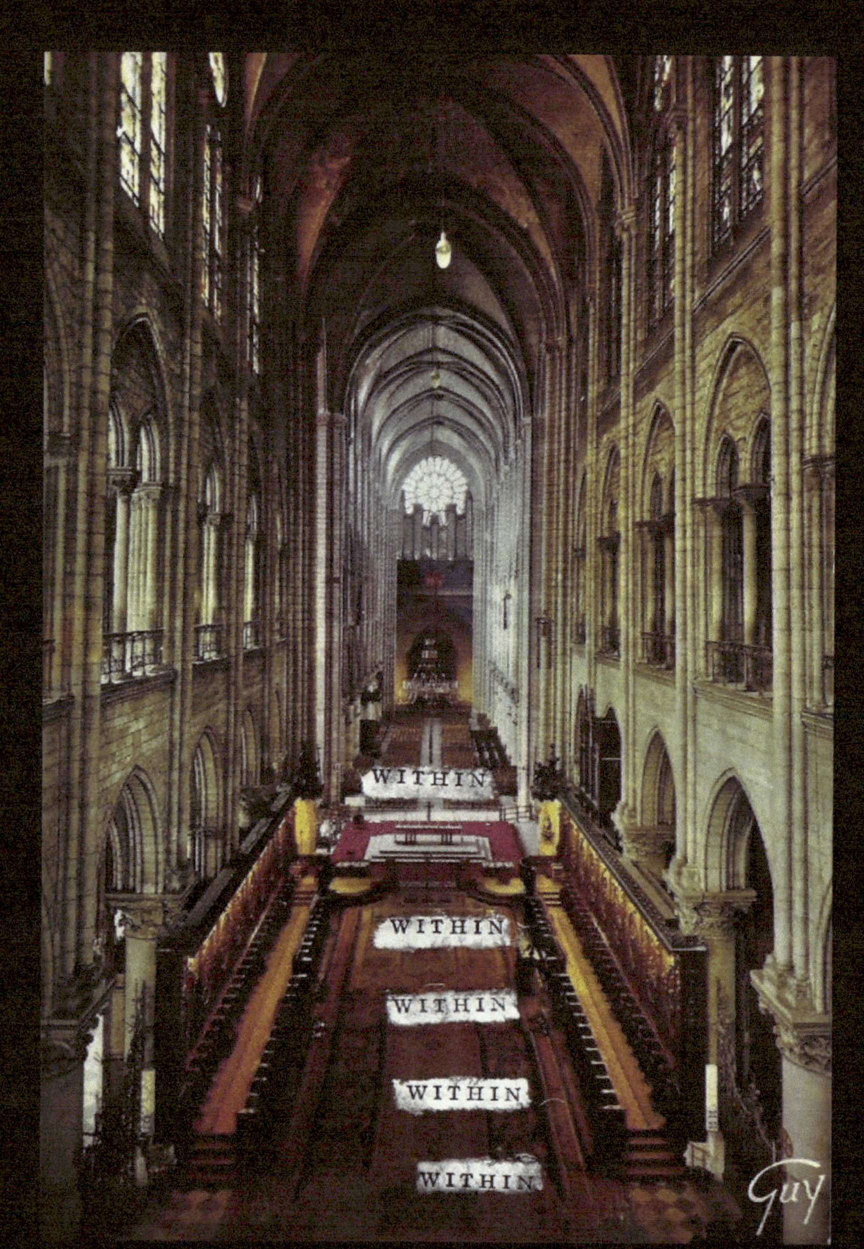

WITHIN
WITHIN
WITHIN
WITHIN
WITHIN
Guy

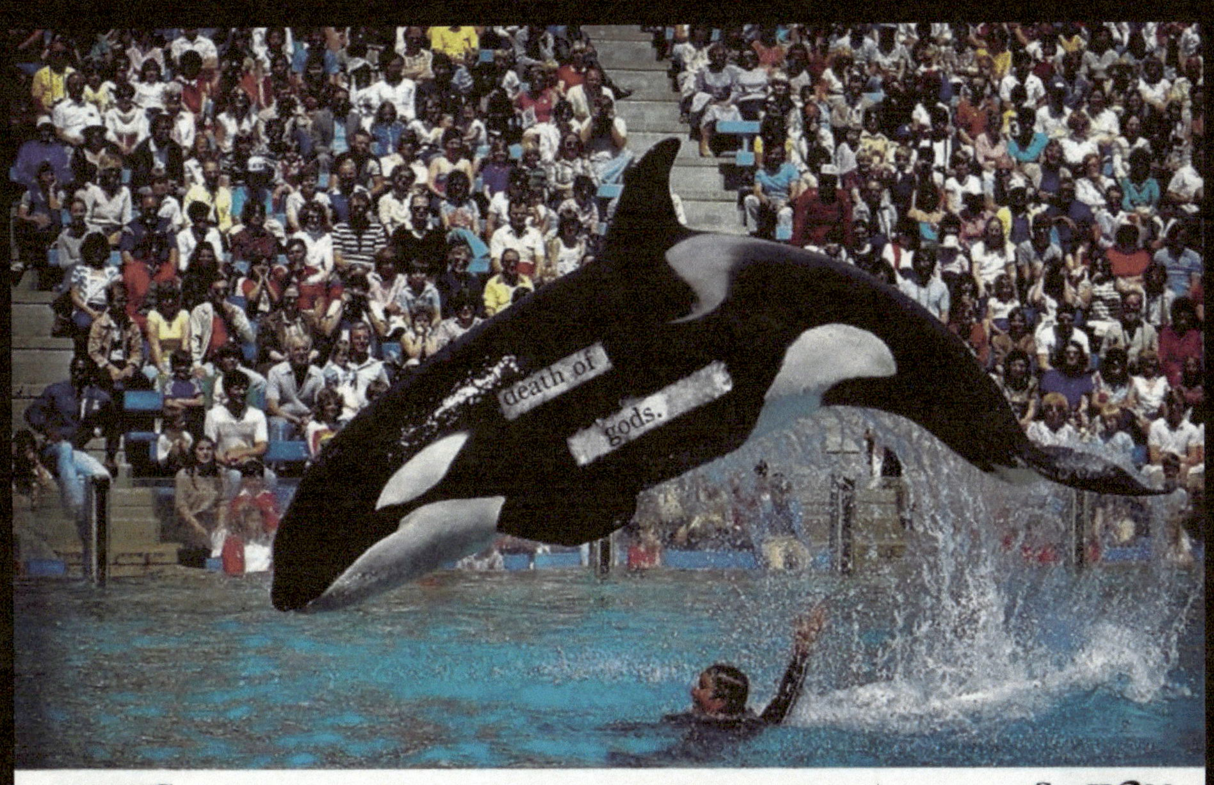
death of
gods.
SHAMU™
Sea World®

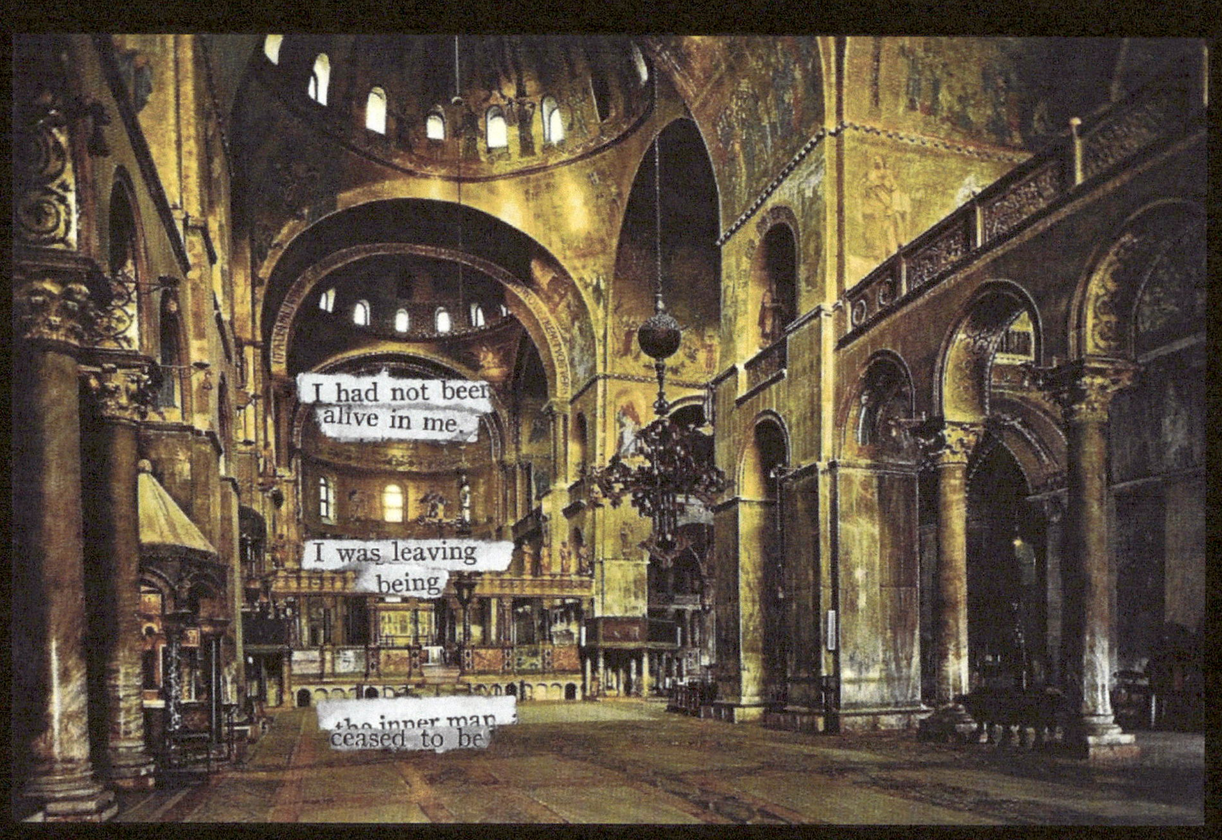
I had not been
alive in me.
I was leaving
being
the inner man
ceased to be

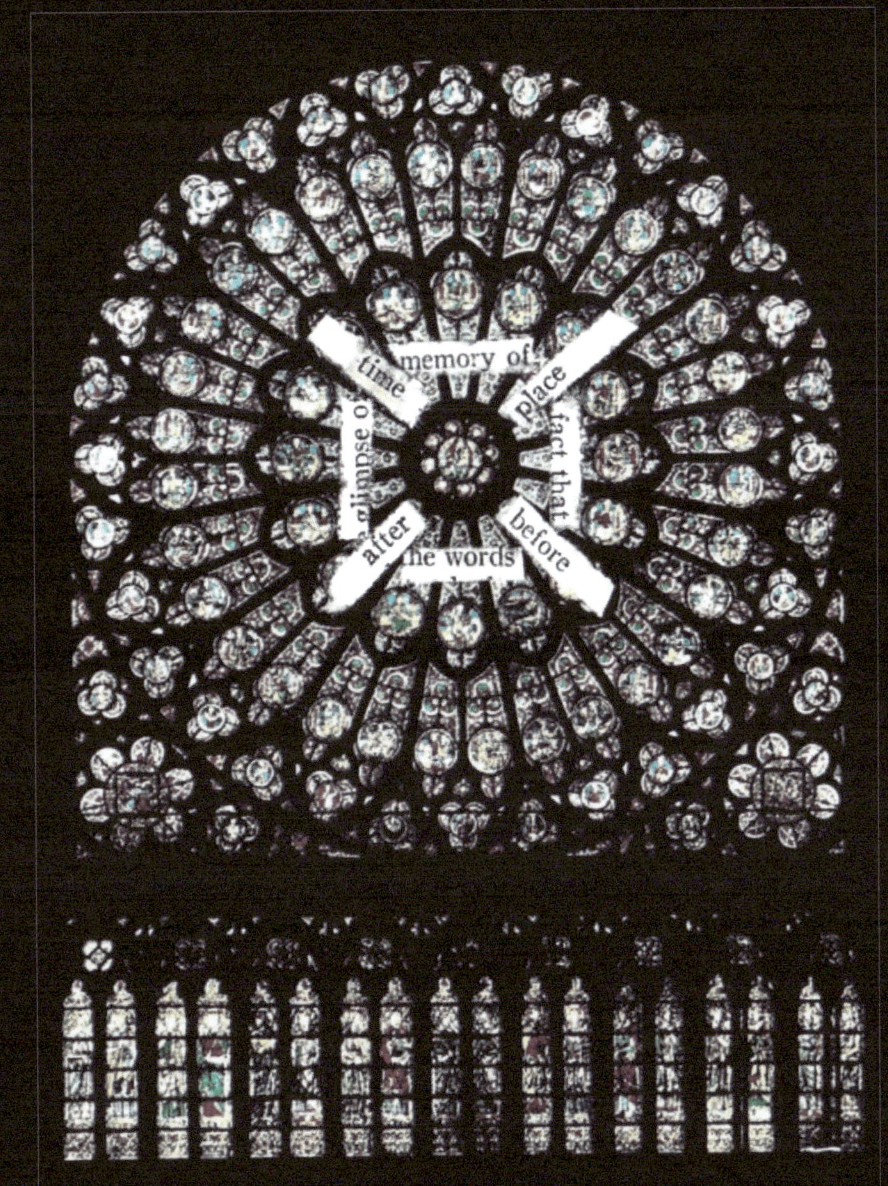
memory of
time
place
glimpse o
fact that
after
before
the words

...P.S. That is all

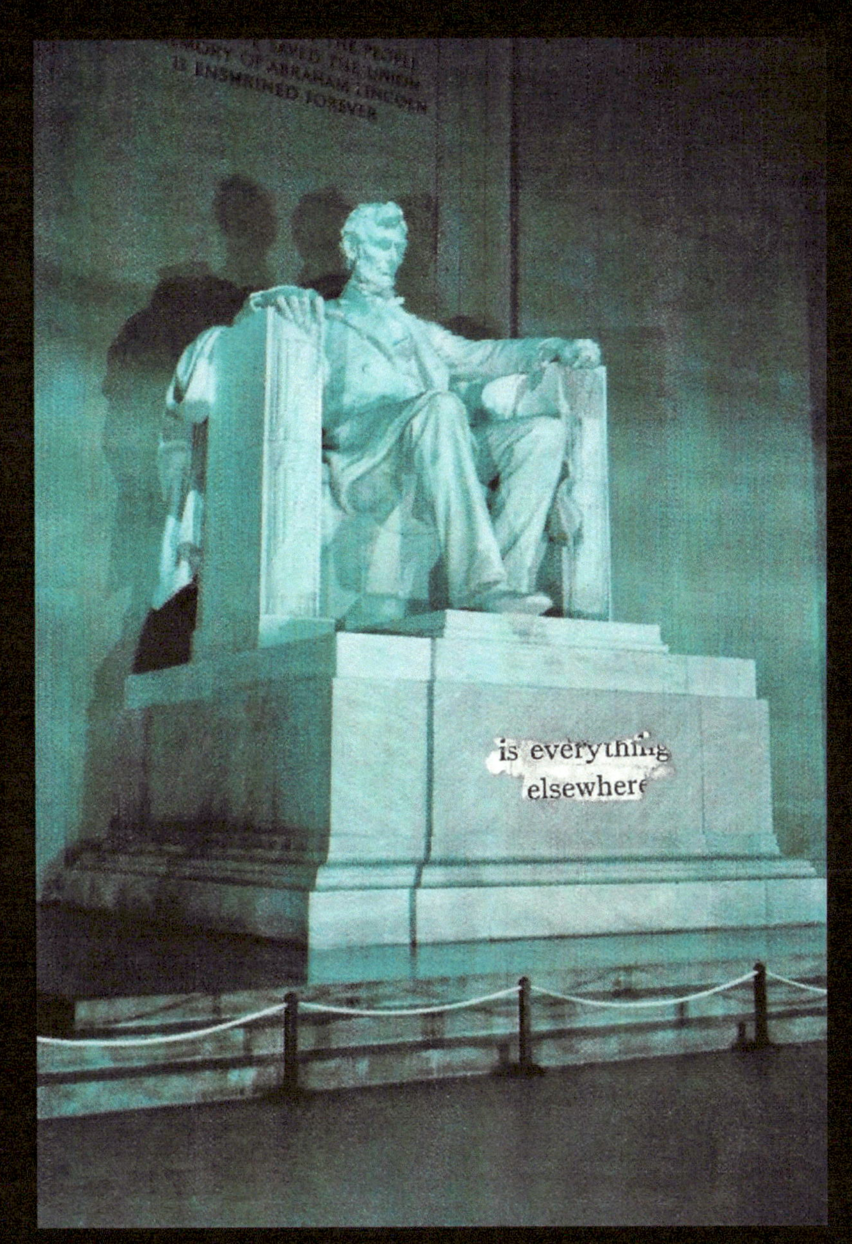
SAVED THE PEOPLE
MEMORY OF ABRAHAM LINCOLN
IS ENSHRINED FOREVER
is everything
elsewhere

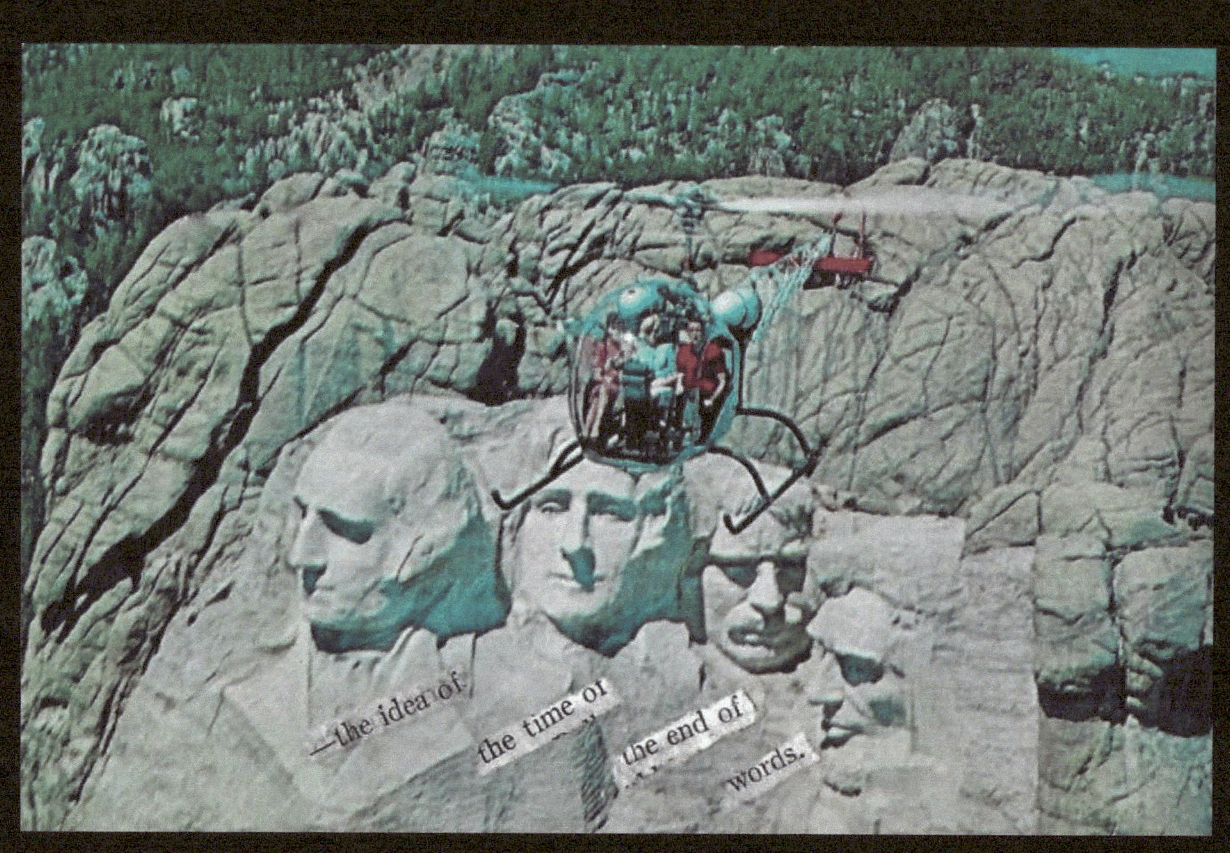
the idea of
the time of
the end of
words.

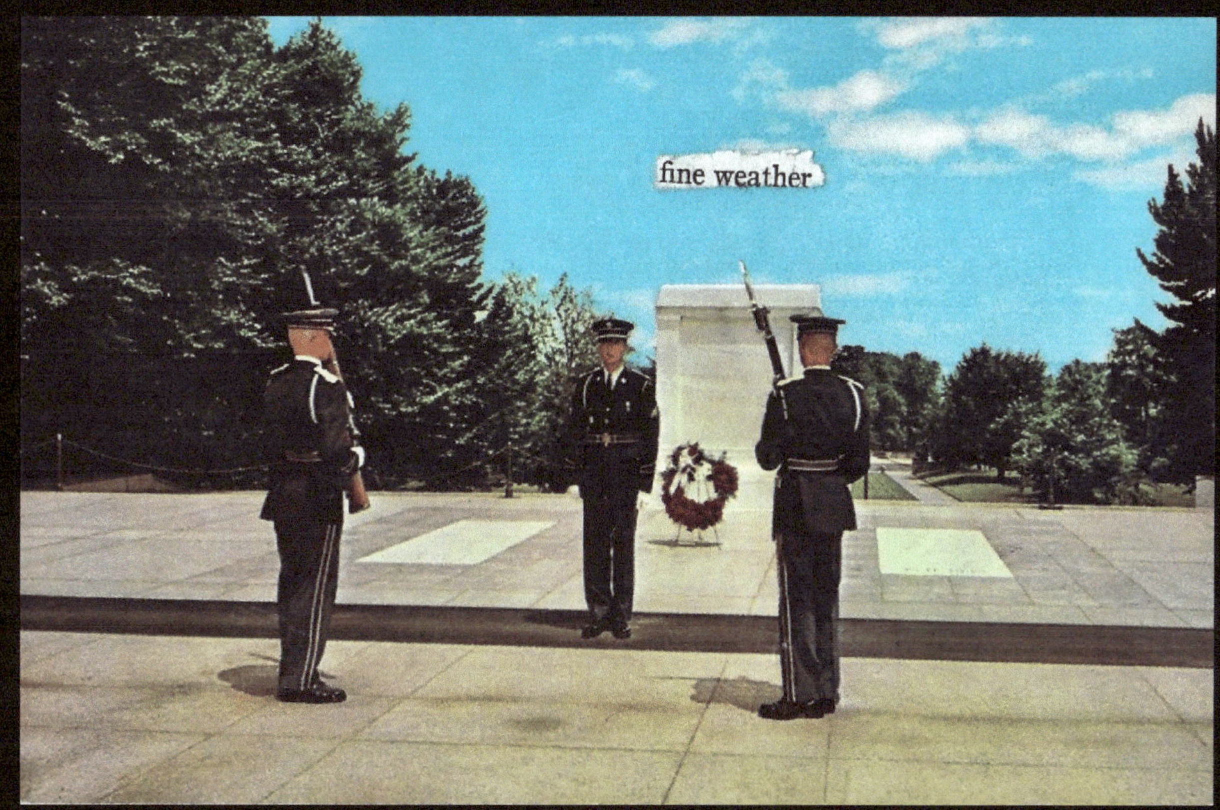
fine weather

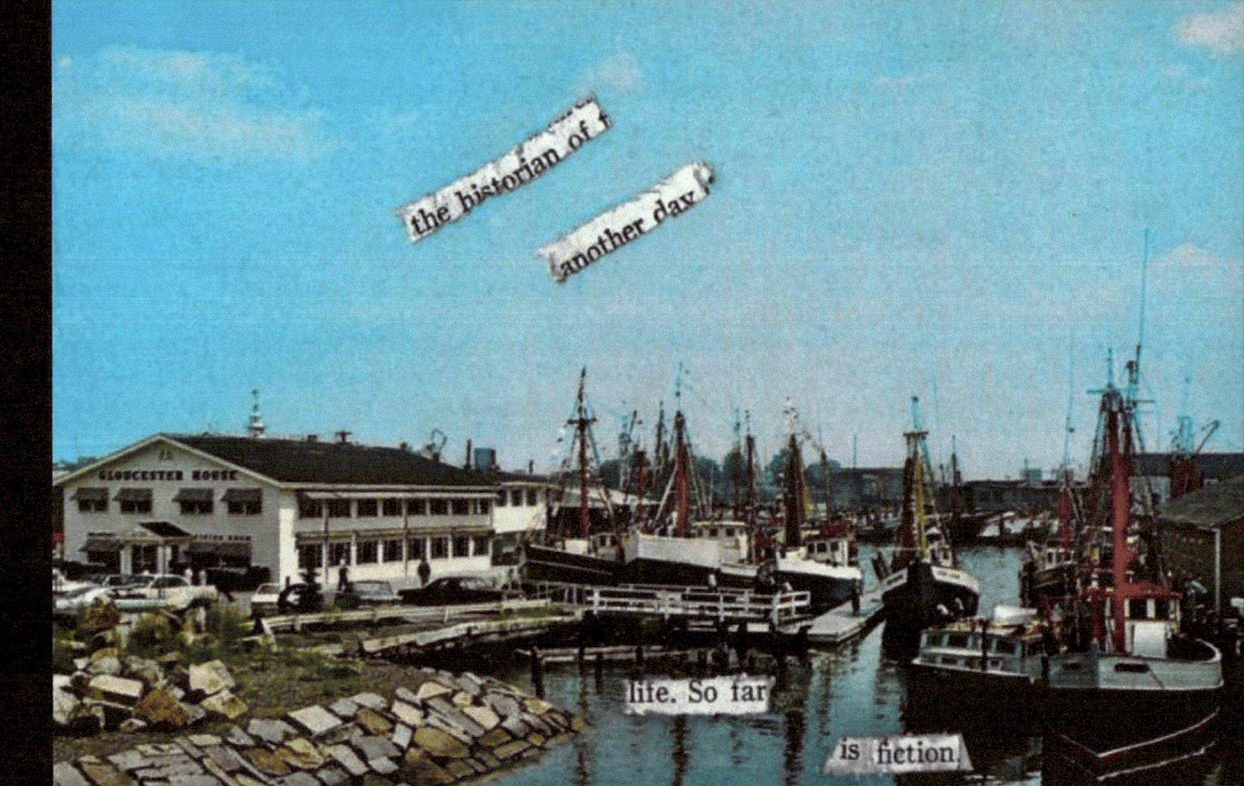
the historian of
another day
life. So far
is fiction.
GLOUCESTER HOUSE

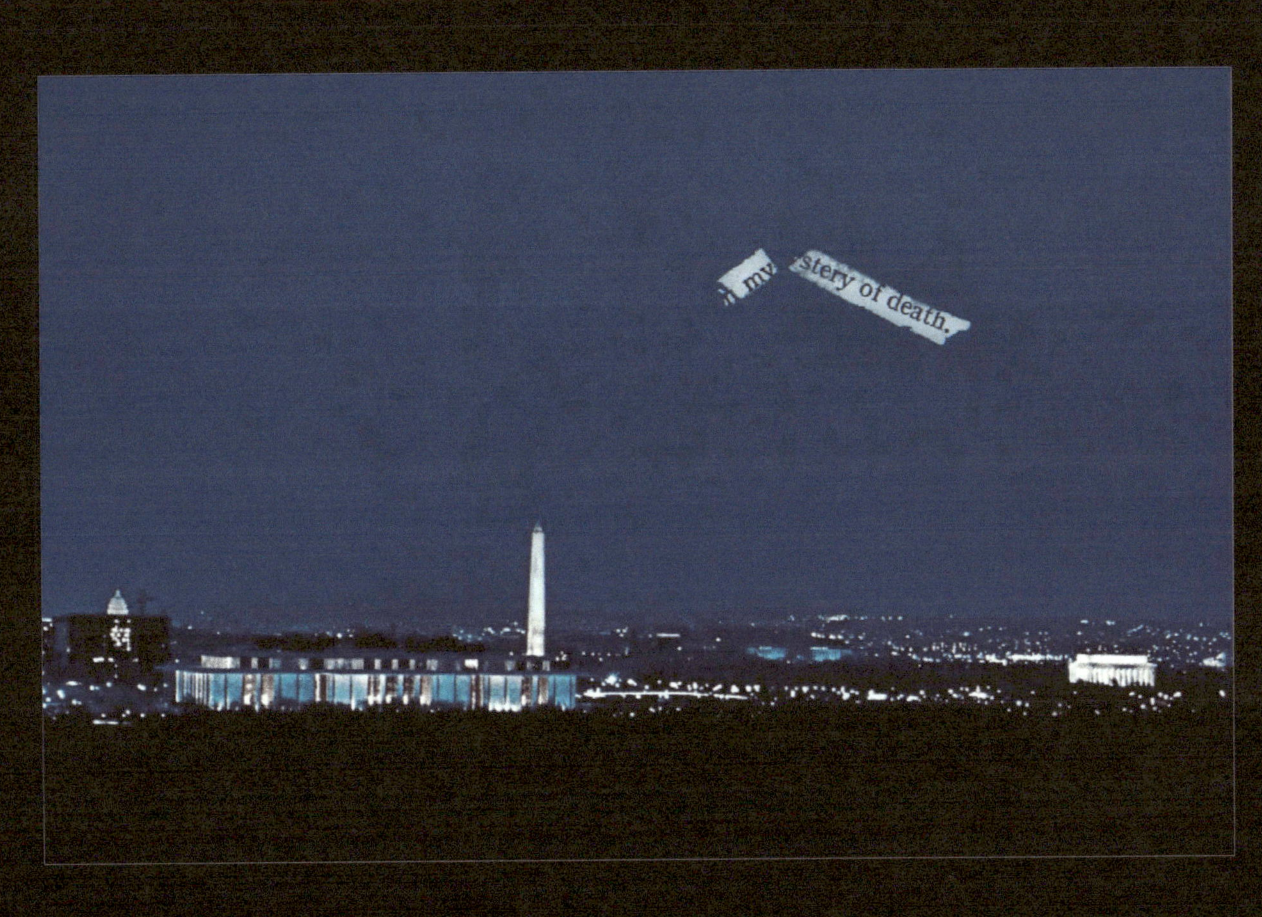
mystery of death.

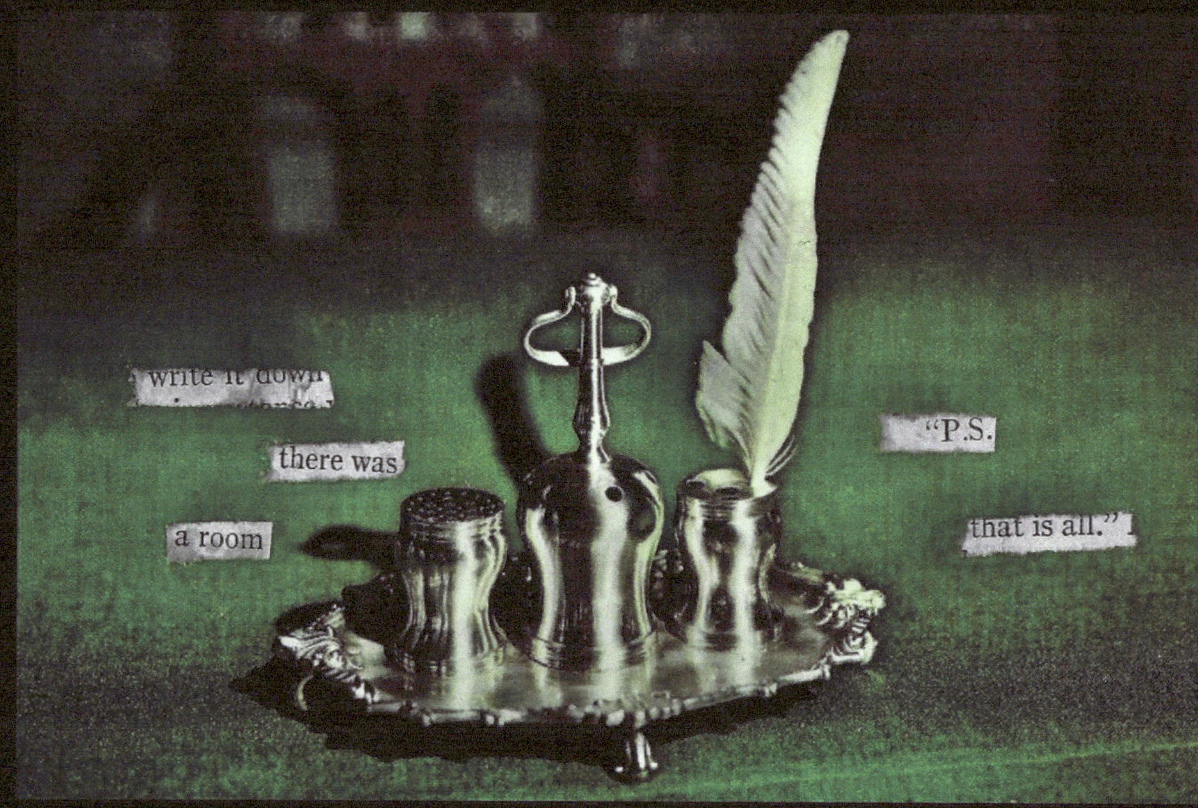
write it down
there was
a room
"P.S.
that is all."

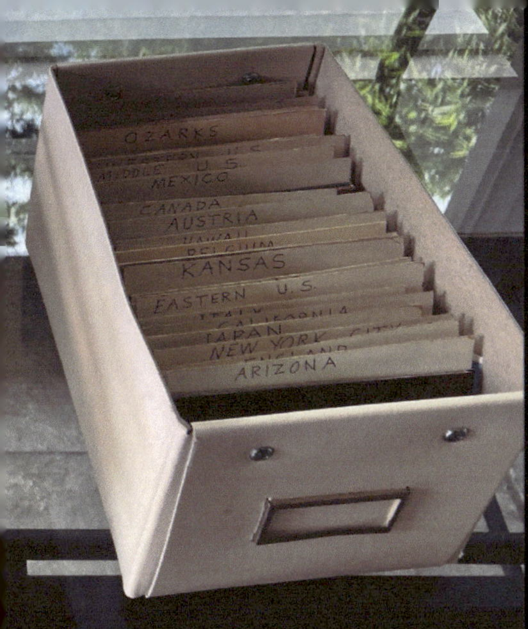

The box of catalogued postcards

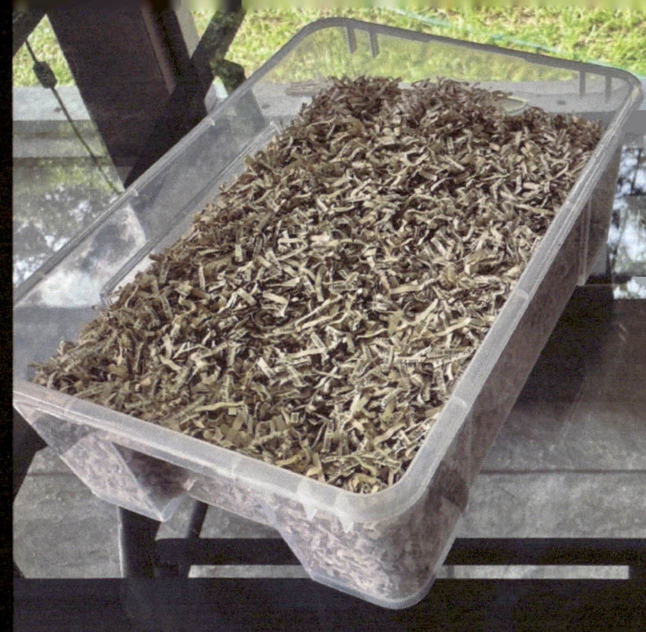

A container of shredded Proust

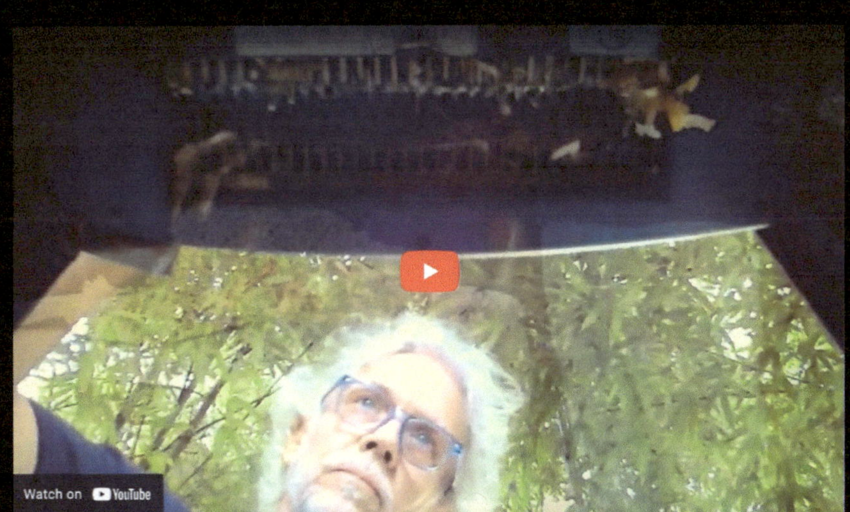

"Shredding Proust"
In conjunction with the exhibition "Routine Maintenance," at the University of North Florida Gallery of Art,
a 24-hour virtual performance festival on September 24th, 2021.
https://www.youtube.com/watch?v=vU3bzDzfZFM&t=1s

Clark Lunberry is a Professor in the Department of English at the University of North Florida,
in Jacksonville, Florida.

Many thanks to those early supportive eyes of Carolyne Ali-Khan, Mark Ari, Jefree Shalev, and Michael Wiley;
and, at Tofu Ink Arts Press, the passion and commitment of Brian Jacobs and Joseph Lee.